The State We're In: Washington

Your guide to state, tribal & local government

Jill Severn, author

Leslie Hoge, graphic designer

Karen Verrill, project manager

Produced and published by

The League of Women Voters of Washington
Education Fund

2004

ACKNOWLEDGEMENTS

The League of Women Voters of Washington Education Fund, the author and the designer thank the following people who generously contributed information, expertise, editorial advice, and drafts of various features.

Catherine Ahl; Gerry Alexander, Chief Justice, Washington State Supreme Court; Justin Amorratanasuchad; Chris Bulloch; Darrell Cochrane, Senior Environmental Health Specialist, Thurston County Environmental Health Department; Cary Collins; Wendy Ferrell, Communications Manager, Office of the Administrator of the Courts; David Hastings, Chief Archivist, Washington State Archives; Denny Heck; Judy Hedden; Bruce Henne; Cynthia Iyall, Economic Development Specialist, Nisqually Tribe; Gordon James, Chair, Skokomish Tribe; Colleen Jollie, Tribal Liaison, Washington State Department of Transportation; Trixanna Koch; Joan Koenig, Executive Assistant, Island Enterprises; Kara Kondo; Sue Lean; Kyle Taylor Lucas, Executive Director, Governor's Office of Indian Affairs; Steve Lundin; Trudy Marcellay, Regional Program Manager, Indian Policy & Support Services, Washington State Department of Social and Health Services; Darlene Madenwal; Jocelyn Marchisio; Nancy Miller; Maureen Morris, Deputy Director, Washington State Association of Counties; Madison Murphy; Rich Nafziger, Chief Clerk, House of Representatives; Caleb Perkins, Program Supervisor of Social Studies/ International Education, Office of the Superintendent of Public Education; Luis Prado, Graphic Designer, Washington State Department of Natural Resources; Andy Robertson; Steve Robinson, Policy Analyst, Northwest Indian Fisheries Commission; Bruce Sanford, Species Specialist, Washington State Department of Fish and Wildlife; Dan Silver; Daniel Hoyt Smith, MacDonald Hoague and Bayless; Joan Smythe; Deborah Sosa, Tribal Liaison, Washington State Department of Health; Hugh Spitzer, Foster Pepper & Shefelman PLLC; Lisa Steppe; Alice Stolz; Betty Tabbutt; Natalie Toevs; Peggy Ushakoff, Technician, Dept of Fish and Wildlife; Gordon Verrill; Robert Whitener Jr., CEO and President, Island Enterprises; Mike Woodall, G.I.S. Analyst, Washington State Department of Ecology; Susan Zemick, Public Awareness & Marketing Manager, Washington State Department of Health

table of contents

photo credits and information can be found in their respective chapters

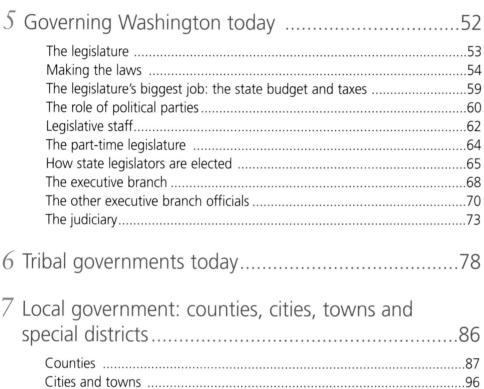

"With great power comes great responsibility."

Spiderman

Foreword

My father recently died. Understandably, I often find myself thinking about him and his life's remarkable journey. It is a familiar story. His grandparents were immigrants. When he began school in rural South Dakota in 1921, he spoke no English, only German. The Great Depression catapulted him out of school in the ninth grade in an attempt to help save the family's hard scrabble farm. A few years later, survival came in the form of federal public works projects. Still later, he answered his country's call to duty in World War II. Afterwards, he began driving truck (which he did for 37 years), and moved to the emerging suburbs to raise his four children.

Although I do not recall a single instance of his leading a family discussion about current events, I do remember that he read two newspapers every day from front to back. He was a bit stoic in the sense we sometimes think of those of German background, but he occasionally expressed a healthy skepticism of large institutions. I also recall that no matter what the circumstance, he never missed voting – for anything, be it a school measure or the presidency.

In other words, my father worked hard, played by the rules, and sacrificed to make a better life for his children.

What does all this have to do with the outstanding book that follows? Everything. This book is about the civic community that is shared by all of us and binds us together. It is about the most important and basic information required to "be in the game." It is about the rights and responsibilities inherent in the "greatest experiment" ever undertaken. It is about the tremendous intergenerational responsibility that has characterized our living, breathing, dynamic way of governing ourselves. Finally, it is about as well written as is possible.

That's no surprise. The author, Jill Severn, is the best writer I have ever had the privilege to know personally. This is her voice. It is well worth listening to. I think so much of it, that were it mine, I would dedicate it to my dad.

Denny Heck
FORMER STATE REPRESENTATIVE AND MAJORITY LEADER
CHIEF OF STAFF TO GOVERNOR BOOTH GARDNER
CO-FOUNDER & PRESIDENT, TVW

There are many ways for you to be involved in your government.

photos clockwise from upper left are courtesy: Washington Education Association; Northwest Indian Fisheries Commission; Bill Wagner and *The Daily News* of Longview, WA; Leslie Hoge Design; photo by Ron Soliman, May 8, 2004, reprinted courtesy *The Olympian*.

The state we're in: Washington

Introduction

This book is about how we govern ourselves. It addresses three very basic questions:

- **What is a government?**

- **Why do we need one?**

- **Why should I care about it?**

By the time you've finished this book, you should be able to answer these questions easily. You will also know enough about state, tribal and local government to be an active citizen – someone who helps keep our democracy alive and healthy.

The most important point to learn about government is that, in a democracy, government belongs to all of us. If we don't like what the government is doing, it's up to us to change it. And if we do like something government is doing, it's up to us to make sure it continues.

Having a democracy is a little bit like having a pet dog. It's a lot of fun, but it's also a big responsibility. It's a living, breathing creature that needs to be nourished, cared for, loved, and disciplined. It can be annoying, expensive and messy. But it's a cherished part of the family, and so, though we often take it for granted, we must never neglect it.

The difference is, of course, that government is bigger, more important, and far more challenging to keep on a leash. That's why learning about government is so important. If we don't keep our government under control, it can end up controlling us.

If we let that happen, we would betray the work, the wisdom, and the sacrifices of the people who came before us. They created the government that we have today so that our generation – and the generations that will follow us – could live in freedom. Now it's our turn to follow in their footsteps.

How Washington got its name

In March 1853, the U. S. Congress passed an Act that established the Washington Territory. (Before then, this area had been part of the Oregon territory, and was often called "North Oregon.") Congress rejected the suggestion that this new territory be called "Columbia." They thought it would be confused with our national capital, Washington, the District of Columbia. Apparently, at that time people had not yet adopted the habit of calling the national capital "Washington, D. C." or simply "Washington."

So they named the new territory "Washington" to honor our nation's first president – and left us with exactly the problem they wanted to avoid!

Fishermen at Celilo Falls, Columbia River

1 How the first people of Washington governed themselves

In the long march of history, "Washington" is a recent creation. For thousands of years before white settlers came, native people lived in this part of the world without creating the boundaries that define our state today.

The pattern of their lives was shaped by the natural world – by where the rivers flowed, where the berries grew, and where the best fishing spots were located. Washington's first people didn't plant crops or build factories; they fished, hunted, and gathered wild plants for food. They made their homes, their clothing, and everything else they needed from the materials that nature provided.

drawing courtesy Governor's Mansion Foundation

They knew how to harvest fish without harming future fish runs. They knew how to burn prairie lands to keep them open, so that the camas plant whose roots they ate would flourish. They managed the natural world, but they also considered themselves part of it.

During the spring and summer, they often traveled and built summer camps where the best berries or the best hunting was. In the winter, they returned to their winter houses or longhouses, where they spent more time indoors, making baskets, clothing, and other necessities, and telling stories around the fire.

Colville encampment, Chief Joseph's village at pow wow honoring the Nez Perce battle of 1877 at Nespelem, Washington, 1900

Throughout the year, native peoples held special ceremonies to show their appreciation for the bounty that nature provided. They honored the spirits of the fish, the trees, the sun and moon. This powerful connection to the spiritual nature of life was a source of strength and unity.

There were important differences between people on the east and west sides of the Cascades – just as there are today. Much of the east side of the state is drier, more open land, and the climate is hotter in the summer and colder in the winter than the rainy, more heavily forested west side of the state. As you might expect, the people who lived near the coast or around Puget Sound ate more seafood – clams, oysters, and even whale meat, than people who lived on the other side of the Cascade mountains. People in different areas also spoke different languages. What all Washington's first people had in common, though, was that they were very good at catching and preserving salmon. Wild salmon were extremely important to all of Washington's first peoples.

Even though Washington's original cultures and traditions were shaped by differences in climate and location, the way people governed themselves was similar. They didn't write things down, so everything they did involved a lot of talking – and a lot of careful listening. In fact, listening was a very highly-developed skill. Adults taught young people the rules of good behavior by telling stories that gave specific examples of what happened when a person didn't behave the way they should. Young people learned by listening, and by really thinking about what they heard.

When a band or tribe needed to make a decision, they gathered around and talked about what to do. If there was a disagreement, people continued to talk about it until they found a solution everyone could agree on. This is called governing by *consensus*. Sometimes it would take a very long time to reach consensus on a decision, but it was more important for everyone to agree than to make a decision quickly.

Most groups of people had different leaders for different purposes. For instance, one person might be the leader for a hunting trip, but a different person might take the lead in deciding where to build a village. If someone was needed to represent the group

William Shelton carving a story pole, 1920

in dealing with another tribe (or with white explorers or settlers), that might be yet another person. People mostly looked to elders for leadership, because they had more experience and wisdom. In fact, elders were honored and held in high esteem. Sometimes, certain families provided certain kinds of leadership for many generations.

In these societies, no one owned land; that idea never occurred to them. They didn't have hard and fast definitions of who was a member of which tribe, either. They had networks for trading and visiting each other, and people from one band or tribe often married into another. Although each tribal group had its own traditions, its own general territory, and its own ways of doing things, there was plenty of exchange that kept people from becoming isolated.

Chelan women on horseback, Chelan, 1912

Tribal societies in Washington were radically changed by the coming of white settlers in the middle of the 1800s. In just a few years, the settlers, backed by the U. S. government, took over most of the state, and signed treaties with native peoples that required them to give up most of their land. In the place of tribal self-government, the U. S. government asserted its authority.

Swinomish men pose on the beach behind their racing canoe; La Conner, 1895

The traditional ways Washington's people lived and governed themselves were changed forever. But the traditions of Washington's first peoples weren't lost. Even though many of the Indians' spiritual and ceremonial practices were banned for many years by the new settlers' government, they were kept alive, often in secret. On reservations and in Indian communities around the state, those traditions continue to be passed from one generation to the next. Today, many tribes blend ancient traditions with modern ways of governing. Indians often credit their deeply spiritual traditions with giving them the strength to survive the overwhelming force of white settlers, and the many twists and turns of U. S. policy towards native peoples.

Today, Indian self-government, traditions and culture are experiencing a dramatic comeback. A series of court decisions and changes in national and state policy have affirmed the rights spelled out in the treaties and stimulated the growth and development of tribal self-determination. These decisions were won by many years of determined effort by Indian people and their allies. Today, tribal governments are growing and changing, and taking on important new roles and responsibilities. Tribal governments have become more and more important not just to Indians, but to all of us, because they are involved in issues such as saving wild salmon, protecting the health of rivers and streams, managing urban growth, improving education, and creating jobs.

2 The design of today's democracy

Democracy is the idea that people should have control over their government. This is the opposite of government having control of the people. In societies where there is one absolute ruler – a king, or a dictator – all power is held by one person. In a democracy, all power is held by the people.

In a democracy, people control government by voting. When our country was founded, the idea that all people should be able to vote was considered quite radical. The people who wrote the constitution thought they were going pretty far just by giving the right to vote to all white men who owned land. This was a huge change for a people who had been ruled by a king who lived far across the ocean.

Over the years, the right to vote has been expanded to include people who don't own land, African-Americans, women, Native Americans, and immigrants of all races who choose to become citizens. Today, it seems obvious to us that everyone is equal,

portrait of George Washington by Rembrandt Peale, in the Governor's Mansion Olympia, WA

courtesy Governor's Mansion Foundation

and that everyone should have the right to vote. But we need to remember that this was not always so, and that the right to vote is something that many generations of Americans struggled hard to create for us.

Universal suffrage – the right of everyone to vote – is the foundation of democracy, but in a complex society like ours, people cannot vote on everything. We have to choose people to do the work of governing for us. That's why we elect people to represent us. This is called *representative democracy*. (When people vote on everything, it's called *direct democracy*.)

The basic principles of our system of government are spelled out in our nation's constitution, which was adopted when our country was founded over 200 years ago. The constitution sets the basic rules for how government should work. A series of amendments to the constitution called the *Bill of Rights* defines the rights of citizens.

". . .we here resolve that these dead shall not have died in vain — that this nation, under God, shall have a new birth of freedom — and that government of the people, by the people, for the people, shall not perish from the earth."

ABRAHAM LINCOLN'S
GETTYSBURG ADDRESS, 1863

Different kinds of government

We have three basic levels of government: national, state, and local.

• **Our national government** deals with issues that affect our whole nation. This includes managing our relationships with other countries, protecting the U. S. from attack, making national laws, and providing programs and services for all Americans.

• **Our 50 state governments** – and the governments of territories governed by the U. S., like Puerto Rico, Guam and American Samoa – deal with issues that affect the people of their state or territory.

• **Our local governments** make laws and provide services to people within counties, cities and towns.

Tribal governments are also an important part of the United States. In every state, including Washington,  tribes govern the native people who live on the reservations created when their ancestors signed treaties with the federal government.

art courtesy of Northwest Indian Fisheries Commission

State and local governments are based on the same democratic ideas as our national government. Tribal governments are usually based partly on the national model described in our constitution, and partly on the traditional ways tribes governed themselves before settlers came.

Our constitution is the foundation of our democracy. It represents a very careful balance between *individual liberty* and the *common good.* Our constitution protects our freedom to pursue our own dreams and choose our own beliefs, but, at the same time, it calls on citizens and elected leaders to put the common good – the welfare of everyone – ahead of our own interests.

Separation of powers

American democracy has three branches of government – the legislative branch, the executive branch, and the judicial branch. By balancing power among three branches of government, we assure that power is shared, and that no one person or branch of government has absolute authority.

Human beings are far from perfect, and we often have a hard time resisting the temptation to abuse power. We also need stability in our government so that people and businesses can plan for the future. That's why American democracy *spreads power around* rather than giving a lot of power to one elected leader.

American democracy has three branches of government – **the legislative branch, the executive branch,** and **the judicial branch**. By balancing power among three branches of government, we assure that power is shared, and that no one person or branch of government has absolute authority.

• ***At the federal or national level, the legislative branch makes laws,*** and decides how to spend the federal taxes that all of us pay. The legislative branch consists of the Senate and the House of Representatives. (Together, the House and Senate are called the *Congress*.) The people of each state elect two Senators, no matter how big or small the state is. But the number of Representatives each state elects to the House of Representatives depends on how many people live there. (For example, Washington currently has nine Representatives; California has 52.)

• ***The president, who is the head of the executive branch,*** can approve or reject (*veto*) the laws Congress makes. If the President vetoes a law, the Congress can cancel (*override*) the veto by passing the law again, but this time two-thirds of them (not just a *simple majority* of half plus one) have to vote for it.

The president is also the boss for most national government agencies, and is the Commander in Chief of the military.

• The most important part of the judicial branch is the Supreme Court. There are nine Justices on the Supreme Court. They are appointed for life by the President, but the Senate has to vote to approve of the President's appointments. Because Supreme Court Justices are appointed for life, they don't have to worry about losing their jobs if they make decisions that someone doesn't like. Their primary duty is to make sure that the laws passed by Congress, states, and local governments respect the basic principles laid out in our nation's constitution. If the Supreme Court decides a law is unconstitutional, it can throw the law out. The Supreme Court can also rule on cases about whether police and other government agencies – including the president – respect the constitutional rights of citizens.

This system of government is not designed to be efficient and fast; it is designed to be careful and slow. A new law has to be debated and voted on by the legislative branch, approved by the executive branch, and, if anyone challenges it, upheld by our judicial branch.

There is often tension and conflict between the three branches of government. Presidents sometimes get angry when the Senate doesn't approve their appointments to the Supreme Court. Congress doesn't like it when a President vetoes a law they've passed. But because everyone agrees with the basic rules set out in the constitution, these conflicts don't get out of hand.

Photodisc photo

Mt. Rushmore features four presidents carved into a mountainside. Can you name all four?

This basic idea – the idea of *separation of powers* into the three branches of government – is reflected in the way state and local governments are organized, too. But state and local governments vary in the way they do this. Nebraska, for instance, has only one legislative body instead of two. And in our state, we elect the members of our state Supreme Court rather than letting the Governor (the head of our executive branch) appoint them.

Many local governments combine some of the functions of the legislative and executive branches because they are just too small to maintain three separate branches. But the basic principle of spreading power around is a universal feature of American governance. It is often called a system of *checks and balances*.

The rule of law

A cornerstone of American government is the idea of having a "government of laws rather than a government of men." This means that our government is guided by the law, not by what one person – or one group of people – wants to do. Our laws are intended to apply to everyone equally. No one is supposed to get special treatment, no matter how rich or powerful they may be. And the power of all government officials is limited to what the law says they can do.

Majority rule, minority rights

When our nation was founded, the people who wrote our constitution worked hard to balance two ideas. The first – majority rule – is the idea that the ultimate power in a democracy is vested in the people. When we elect leaders, the majority of the people – that is, 50% plus one or more – determines who wins.

The second idea relates to "the rule of law." The idea is that the majority shouldn't be able to violate the rights of a minority. Like the idea of the separation of powers, this idea recognizes that people are imperfect. Sometimes the majority of people are prejudiced against a certain group of people – people of a different race or religion, or people who have different political beliefs, for instance. Our political system is designed

to protect minorities by providing all citizens with the same rights, and by giving the Supreme Court the power to strike down any law, no matter how popular, if it violates the rights of even one person. These ideas are reflected in the U. S. constitution's Bill of Rights.

Federalism

The word *federalism* describes the division of responsibility between state governments and our national government. When our country was founded, it was made up of 13 colonies that had been created by England. As our national constitution was being written, there were lots of arguments about how much power they would have when they became states, and how much power the national government would have. In the end, the general idea was that the federal government would make rules about things that crossed state lines, and states would be responsible for everything else. So, for instance, states are responsible for education, but the national government is responsible for defending our nation from attack.

Not all of the arguments about state versus national government power were really settled when the constitution was written. In the history of the U. S., the relative power of state and federal governments has continued to change. During the civil rights movement of the 1960s for instance, southern states argued that they had "states' rights" to discriminate against African-Americans. After a long series of debates and court cases, it was decided that they did not.

Immigration

People who come to the U. S. from other countries are called immigrants. Sometimes people say that the U. S. is a *nation of immigrants,* since all of us except Indians are descendants of *immigrants*. Today, about 11% of the people in the U. S. were born in another country.

Photodisc photo

Some immigrants come to this country because they are fleeing from war in their home country. Some come because they might be jailed or even killed for their political or religious beliefs or their race. These people are called *refugees*, because they are seeking *refuge* – a safe place. But most immigrants come to join family members who are already here, or because they want better jobs and more opportunities for their children. Sometimes immigrants come because there is a shortage of people for certain jobs or professions – nurses, for instance, or computer professionals, or farm workers.

The federal government sets the number of immigrants that can come to the U. S. every year. Often when people in other countries apply to come here, they have to wait many years before they get permission from the federal government. Many never get permission. If they come to the U. S. without getting permission first, or if they stay longer than they have permission to, they are considered *illegal immigrants*. There are probably several million illegal immigrants in the U. S. today. (No one knows the exact number.)

Most illegal immigrants come to this country because they are poor and they need jobs. And lots of American employers hire them, even though it is against the law to do so. There is a constant conflict about this. Some people think all illegal immigrants should be rounded up and sent back to their home countries. Other people think that some or all the illegal immigrants in the country should be given *amnesty* – meaning they should be given permission to stay, and be made *legal* immigrants, because employers need them, and because they make an important contribution to the American economy by working and paying taxes.

Women immigrating from Japan

photo courtesy Seattle Betsuin Archives

Only legal immigrants can apply to become American citizens. To become a citizen, an immigrant has to live in this country for at least five years. Then they have to fill out an application form, pay a fee, be interviewed by a U. S. official, and pass a test to show that they have learned to read, write and speak English; that they know some U. S. history; and that they understand how American government works.

The 20th Annual Naturalization Ceremony on July 4th, 2004 at the Seattle Center, where many people became U. S. citizens.

All children born in the U. S. are citizens by birth. If adults come to this country illegally and then have children while they are here, the children are U. S. citizens because they were born in this country. If their parents are here illegally, or if the parents commit a crime, they can be *deported*, or sent back to the country they came from. But what happens to the children? Legally, they have a right to stay here – but to exercise that right, they might have to be separated from their own Mom and Dad.

Immigration also gets complicated when it comes to deciding what government services people get. Illegal immigrants pay taxes, but they don't get the same benefits as other taxpayers. They can't get welfare, government-paid health insurance, or help if they get hurt and can't work. (Even legal immigrants can't get most welfare benefits.)

People argue about this a lot. If a woman is a poor illegal immigrant, and she's going to have a baby, should the government pay for her medical care? Some people say no, because she broke the law by coming here illegally. Other people say yes, because the baby will be a U. S. citizen, and we want that child to be born healthy.

People have similar arguments about whether kids who are illegal immigrants should be able to go to school. Some people say that U. S. citizens shouldn't have to pay to educate kids who are here illegally. But the U. S. Supreme Court has said that the kids shouldn't be punished for something their parents did. They say that educating all kids is the best and only way to make sure that they can get jobs and pay taxes when they grow up. (Washington's state constitution says we should educate all children "residing" in our state, not just those who are citizens.)

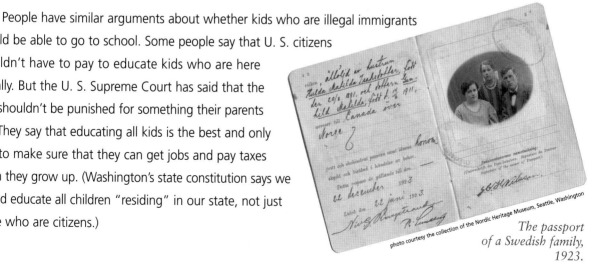

The passport of a Swedish family, 1923.

In the presidential election of November 2000, 111 million people, or 55%, of the voting-age population voted. That means that almost half of the eligible voters let someone else make important decisions for them. Only about 65% of people eligible to vote are registered to vote. Women, married people, and older people are more likely to vote.

In Washington, 80% of people eligible to vote were registered in 2000, and 76% of all of those registered to vote actually did vote. So in our state, 61% of people eligible to vote did. Washinton was ranked 19th in the country in voting rates.

Some reasons given by registered non-voters for not voting in the 2000 election include: too busy (21%), illness or emergency (15%), not interested (12%), forgot (4%). Yikes!

Voters in the 2000 election

□ all U.S. voters	■ Washington state voters

	percent of the voting age that is registered to vote	percent of those registered to vote and did vote	percent of the voting age that did vote
all U.S.	64%	86%	55%
Washington	80%	76%	61%

source: U.S. Census Bureau, Current Population Survey, November 2000.

Becoming a citizen is important because only citizens are allowed to vote, and only citizens have the absolute right to stay in this country, no matter what. Even legal immigrants who have lived here for many years can be deported if they have not become citizens. Some young people have been deported for drug charges or stealing, even though they lived legally in the U. S. since they were babies.

The role of citizens

Elections

The most basic way people in a democracy exercise political power is by voting in elections. We elect the people who represent us – the members of city or tribal councils, county commissions, state governors and legislators, and the President and the Congress of the United States. And if we don't like what they do, we can vote them out of office.

We also vote on specific issues. For instance, in Washington, local communities vote on how much we are willing to pay in taxes to support public schools. We also vote sometimes on special issues, like whether we want to pay extra taxes to build sports stadiums. And we vote on amendments to our state constitution.

Initiatives and referenda

In the early 20th century, people wanted to make doubly sure that citizens kept control over our government. So even though our state government has the same checks and balances as our national government, Washington voters amended the state constitution to build in an extra "check" – the power of citizens to bypass the legislature, write a proposed law and have the people vote on it. This is called an *initiative*.

To pass an initiative, a citizen or group of citizens must get a large number of people to sign petitions asking for a proposed law to be put on the ballot. If enough people sign, the proposed law can go to the legislature, or directly to the ballot. (The number of people who have to sign an initiative is 8% of the number who voted in the last election for governor.)

If an initiative goes to the legislature, the legislature can pass it, and it becomes law. The legislature can also write an alternative measure, and put both the original initiative and their proposed alternative on the ballot of the next election. If the legislature doesn't do anything, the initiative still goes to the voters at the next election. If a majority of people vote for it, it becomes law. (Even if an initiative passes, the state supreme court can throw it out if it violates the state constitution. And if it violates the U. S. constitution, the U. S. supreme court can throw it out.)

People in Washington also vote on referenda. A *referendum* is a law passed by the state legislature, but *referred* to the voters. Sometimes the legislature itself refers a measure to the ballot to see if the majority of voters agrees that it should become law. But sometimes a citizen or group of citizens doesn't like a law passed by the legislature. If they can get enough people to sign a petition, they can get the law put on the ballot. (The number of people who have to sign the petitions is 4% of the number of people who voted in the last election for governor.) Then if the majority of people vote against it, the new law is thrown out.

photo courtesy Tim Eyman

One person's opinion makes a difference

Tim Eyman, who lives in Mukilteo, thought that taxes in Washington were too high, so he organized several initiative campaigns. He raised money, made petitions, persuaded thousands of people to sign them, and got measures on the ballot to reduce taxes.

Other examples of successful initiatives

• In 1977, voters passed an initiative that removed the sales tax on food. This was an initiative directly to the people.

• In 1988, voters passed an initiative to clean up dangerous toxic waste sites. It was an initiative to the legislature. The legislature drafted an alternative, so both the legisla-ture's version and the original version were on the ballot. Voters chose the original version.

photo courtesy of Gayle Rieber Photography

photo by Ron Soliman, February 3, 2004, reprinted courtesy *The Olympian*

*Local communities vote on how much they are willing
to pay in taxes to support public schools*

Running for office

Another important way citizens participate in government is by running for public office. Most people who decide to do this start by running for a local office, such as being a school board member, or a city council member. When they are more experienced, and more people know them and support them, they run for higher offices. But this is not always true; sometimes a person who has never been involved in government decides to run for governor or the U. S. Congress.

People who run for office need money to finance their campaigns. They have to buy campaign signs, publish brochures to let people know what they stand for, and sometimes buy advertising in newspapers or on radio or TV. If they are running for a statewide office, they also need money to travel around the state to campaign.

Candidates for public office usually ask the people who support them to donate money for their campaigns, although sometimes rich people finance their own campaigns.

(There's more information about running for office in Chapter 5.)

The role of money in election campaigns is very controversial. In a democracy, we want everyone to have an equal chance to be heard. And we don't want individuals, unions or corporations that have a lot of money to have more than their share of influence in an election. We don't want our elected officials to feel that they have to vote the way their campaign contributors want them to. So we have rules about who can give, and how much they can give. And every few years, we pass more rules. But hardly anyone believes that we have found the perfect solution to this problem.

The most important safeguard we have come up with is the principle of *transparency*, or openness. This means that everyone should be able to find out who gave money to a political campaign, and how much. We have very strict laws that require every candidate and every campaign organization to report their contributions. A special government agency, the Public Disclosure Commission, makes this information available to the public and to reporters. (There's more information about this on page 64.)

Still, campaign financing will always be a subject we debate, both in elections for public office, and in campaigns to pass initiatives and other ballot measures.

Jury Duty

Citizens also serve on juries. A jury is a group of people – usually 12 – who sit in judgment when someone is brought to court and accused of a crime. A judge conducts the trial, but members of the jury have to decide whether the accused person is guilty or innocent. (In civil cases, where one person or business is suing another person or business, juries usually have only six members.)

This is called "jury duty" because it is a duty that comes with being an American citizen.

Advocacy

Having a democracy doesn't mean that our government is perfect. But democracy's flaws are not in the ideas that are the basis for our government; its flaws come from our failure to live up to those ideas.

American history is, in many ways, the story of the struggle of the American people to live up to the ideals set out in the U. S. constitution. Over many years, voting rights have been extended to all citizens, and discrimination against people because of their race or religion has been made illegal. These changes didn't come easily. But these changes were possible because our constitution established the idea of equality as the foundation of our society.

Today, there are still ways in which we fail to live up to the ideas in our constitution. For instance, in today's society, equality depends on everyone getting a good education. But we haven't yet succeeded in reaching this goal. In communities where people don't have very much money, they can't afford to pay enough in taxes to have schools as good as those in richer communities. The result is that kids in poorer communities may not have the same opportunities to learn and succeed.

The important thing to remember, though, is that in a democracy, *people have the power to change these things*. It isn't easy, and it often takes a very long time. But the history of our country – and our state – show that progress is possible.

This progress is possible because we have the right to say what we think, to band together to push for change, and to support or oppose candidates for public office.

We are so used to having these rights that we often forget how important they are. Many Americans don't bother to vote, and don't make their voices heard. But our democratic rights are a lot like our muscles: the more we use them, the stronger they become. If we don't exercise our rights, our democracy becomes weaker.

So, to sum up, American democracy is built on the belief that *we govern ourselves*. This is both our right and our responsibility. That's why it's so important to learn about how our government works.

ADVOCACY:

Promoting a point of view or belief, or working to help a certain group of people. (For instance, someone who tries to get laws passed to help people with disabilities would be advocating for them. The person who does this would be an advocate.)

An example of advocacy

The Arc of Washington State is one example of people using their rights. The Arc is a private, non-profit organization started by the parents of people who have developmental disabilities. (A developmental disability is a condition such as mental retardation that occurs before the age 18.) By banding together, the parents of people with these disabilities have persuaded the government to give them more help, so they can choose whether to live in their own houses or apartments. The Arc of Washington State also helps educate all people about what it's like to have a developmental disability, and why it's important to accept and include people with these disabilities in our schools and communities.

Visit their website at: **www.arcwa.org**

Advocates rally to support the Fircrest Bill, which would help use funds for more community-based services for people with developmental disabilities.

Now people with devlopmental disabilities are more active in their communities, thanks to hard work by citizen advocates.

all photos courtesy The Arc of Washington State unless otherwise noted

Photo by Clara Link, courtesy of The Down Syndrome Community 2004 Calendar, Living it Up!
www.downsyndromecommunity.org

The Medicine Creek Treaty and the story of Leschi and Quiemuth

In late 1854, Governor Stevens gathered some settlers, U. S. government officials, and Indians from various tribes around the south end of Puget Sound at a place near Nisqually called Medicine Creek. He wanted the Indians to sign the treaty right then and there, and he didn't want to give them time to talk about it with the people back in their villages. Most of the Indians didn't want to sign, but they didn't feel they had a choice, because the U. S. army had a lot of men with guns. Enough of the Indians signed (or made Xs next to their names) to make the treaty official. The treaty meant that the Indians had to go live on the reservations that Stevens assigned to them.

The Nisqually and Puyallup Indians were upset by the reservations they were assigned to, because it was on hard, rocky ground, far from the rivers where they had always fished. Two brothers, Leschi and Quiemuth, went to Olympia to try to correct this, but they were labeled "trouble makers" and threatened with arrest. They fled into the foothills of Mt. Rainier. A group of settlers went off to find them.

While the settlers were searching for Leschi and Quiemuth, two U. S. soldiers were killed, and some Indians attacked settlers. Some people blamed Leschi for this, even though others said he was not in the area when these things happened. For ten months, there was fighting between Indians and whites. Then Governor Stevens called for a Peace Council, and promised to create better reservations. When Leschi came to this gathering, he was arrested. Quiemuth also surrendered. Quiemuth was murdered while he was in custody, and no one was ever arrested for this. Leschi was tried for the murder of one soldier. The jury could not come to a decision, and many people insisted he was innocent. A second trial was held, and this time he was declared guilty. He was hanged on February 19, 1858.

Many people – both Indian and settler – were deeply sorry that this happened, and angry that someone they regarded as a great man had been the victim of such a terrible injustice.

In 2004, 150 years after the Medicine Creek treaty was signed, the Washington state legislature passed a memorial calling on the state Supreme Court to acknowledge that Leschi's conviction was an injustice. The memorial also called on the public schools to teach young people the truth about this part of our state's history.

document courtesy Washington State Archives

3 Creating Washington's government

Starting in the 1840s, settlers began to come to Washington. Most of them were white, but a few were African-American or people of mixed race. One party of settlers, for instance, included an African-American man named George Washington Bush. They had gone to Oregon first, but Oregon didn't allow African-Americans to own land, so they traveled north, and settled near Olympia.

In 1854, U. S. President Franklin Pierce sent Isaac Stevens to be the governor of Washington. At that time, Washington was a *territory*. This meant that it was controlled by the federal government, and that the governor worked for the President of the United States. (Washington became a territory in 1853; it became a state in 1889.)

Fort Walla Walla, 1853, from a report published with the results of a railroad survey for the Northern Pacific Railroad.

drawing courtesy Governor's Mansion Foundation

The President wanted Isaac Stevens to negotiate treaties with all the Indians who lived in the Washington territory. The purpose of the treaties was to persuade the Indians to give up most of their lands, so that more white settlers could come and live here. So from 1854-1856, Isaac Stevens traveled all over the state, and persuaded tribes to sign treaties in which the Indians promised to live on *reservations*, or specific pieces of land reserved for them. In many cases, this meant the tribes had to relocate; that is, they had to move from where they usually lived. The tribes were promised small payments for the land they gave up, and they were promised that they could continue to fish, hunt, and gather in their "usual and accustomed places." They were also promised government services such as health care and education.

The white people who wrote the treaties thought that Indians should settle down, learn how to farm, and live like white people. This didn't make much sense to the Indians, who had been fishing, hunting, and moving around freely for thousands of years.

Isaac Stevens and the people who worked for him didn't know very much about the Indians and their way of life, and they didn't take the time to learn, because they were in a hurry to get treaties signed and get all the Indians grouped together on reservations.

There were brief wars between some of the Indians and the federal government over the terms of the treaties. The federal government won.

Within the next few decades, Washington began to fill up with settlers. These settlers wanted Washington to become a state, because then they could form their own state government instead of having a governor appointed by the President.

Writing Washington's constitution

In 1889, 75 men were elected to go to Olympia to write a state constitution. For Washington to become a state, a constitution had to be written and voters had to approve it.

State constitutions are similar to the U. S. constitution, but not exactly the same. Like our national constitution, state constitutions set up the basic organization of

Article I, Section 1 of Washington's state constitution:
All political power is inherent in the people, and governments derive their just powers from the consent of the governed, and are established to protect and maintain individual rights.

government and spell out the rights of citizens. They are the foundation on which government is built. But state constitutions are usually more specific, and have more detail. For instance, our state constitution describes certain services that state government must provide – schools, prisons, and state institutions to care for people who have certain disabilities. The federal constitution doesn't say anything about what services our national government must provide.

State constitutions can also differ from our national constitution in the rights they give to citizens. For instance, Washington's constitution has stronger protections of people's privacy, our right to own guns, and stricter separation between religion and government.

Among the people (called *delegates*) who wrote our constitution there were 22 lawyers, 19 farmers or ranchers, nine store owners or bankers, six doctors, three teachers, and three miners. There were no women in the group because women didn't have the right to vote, except in elections for local school boards. There were also no Indians. At that time, Indians were considered citizens of Indian nations, not citizens of the United States. There were also many Chinese immigrants in Washington, most of whom came here to work in the mines and help build the railroads, but they weren't allowed to become citizens, so they weren't represented either.

Starting on the 4th of July, 1889, the 75 men set to work. They didn't start from scratch. They copied parts of the constitutions of other states, and some sections from an earlier draft of a Washington state constitution that had been written in 1878.

When the legislature ran out of stationery in 1877, a resolution was written on a shingle.

Suffrage: the right to vote.
This is a very confusing word, because it sounds like it's related to "suffer," but it's not. It comes from the Latin word *suffragium*, which also means the right to vote. To make it even more confusing, a *suffrage* can also be a kind of prayer – but that meaning seems to have fallen out of use. Another mystery about the word *suffrage* is why it's almost always used in connection with *women's* right to vote, but rarely in discussions of other people's right to vote.

Big Debates

They had big debates about many issues. For example, they had a long argument about whether the constitution should give women the right to vote. Some thought women should be allowed to vote, but they were afraid that if they said so in the constitution, the voters would reject it, and that would delay Washington becoming a state. Others didn't want women to have the vote because they were afraid women would vote to outlaw alcohol. Companies that made beer and whiskey lobbied to keep women from getting the vote. In the end, the writers of the constitution decided not to put women's suffrage in the constitution.

The Northern Pacific Railroad

They put it on the ballot as a separate measure, and it was defeated by the all-male voters.

The delegates who wrote the constitution also argued about the power of railroads and other big companies. The opening of the railroads in the early 1880s caused a huge population explosion. Railroads opened the state to more settlement, and made it possible for the farmers and ranchers in Eastern Washington to get their products to market. But many farmers and ranchers were angry at the prices the railroads charged. A lot of people also thought the federal government had given away too much public land to the railroads, and that the owners of the railroads and other big companies had too much power and influence over government.

People didn't want the railroads and other big businesses to get control of our state government. So the drafters of our constitution included several things to try to prevent this. They made it illegal for state government to loan money to private companies. They even forbade elected officials from accepting free railroad passes. They insisted on strict separation between private business and state government.

They also had big debates about what to do with the 2.5 million acres of land that the federal government gave to the state. Some of this land was supposed to be used to fund schools and other public buildings. In other states, public lands had been sold off to business owners for a tiny fraction of their real value. People in Washington didn't want that to happen here, so they wrote a strong statement that public lands must never be sold for less than they were worth. (It worked. Today, Washington's state government still owns millions of acres of land, and logging and other activities on that land raise money to help pay for building schools and maintaining our state capitol.)

The biggest arguments, though, were over what to do about tidelands. A lot of businesses had already been established on tidelands. For instance, Henry Yesler had established a sawmill on the tidelands in Seattle. After a lot of debate, it was decided that the state would continue to own the tidelands, but would lease some of them to

photo courtesy Northwest Indian Fisheries Commission

private businesses. (At the time, the writers of the constitution didn't think about the fact that tidelands were part of the "usual and accustomed places" that Indians had been promised rights to fish and gather clams and oysters.)

People's distrust of powerful businesses also influenced the way our state executive branch is organized. The writers of our constitution wanted more than the separation of executive, legislative, and judicial branches of government. They wanted to disperse power even within the executive branch, so that no one official would have too much power. They had seen how easily public officials could be corrupted by wealthy business owners, and they wanted to make sure that our government was honest and accountable to the voters. That's why they created an elected Commissioner of Public Lands to protect the legacy of state-owned land. And that's why we have nine separately elected statewide officials in our executive branch.

Tideland: land that is under water when the tide is in, but not when the tide is out. Tidelands are important for several reasons: oysters, clams and other creatures we eat live there; they provide important habitat for many birds, sea creatures and plants, and tidelands provide access to the ocean (and to Puget Sound and other bays and harbors) that are important for shipping and industry. Many of the tidelands in urban areas have been filled in to make more dry land, and some have been dug up to create deeper water for boats and ships.

University of Washington Libraries, Special Collections, neg A. Curtis 1943

A Quick History of Voting Rights

1776 When the U. S. first became an independent nation, state governments decided who could vote. In most states, only white males who owned property were allowed to vote; in some instances, widows who owned property were allowed to vote, too.

1855 By 1855, all the states had dropped the requirement that voters own property, so all white males could vote.

1868/1870 In 1868, the 14th amendment to the U. S. constitution recognized the citizenship of all African-Americans, and gave male African-Americans the right to vote. The right to vote was made explicit in the 15th amendment. (Still, voting rights were denied to African-Americans in spite of these amendments.)

1890/1920 In 1890, Wyoming became the first state to give women the vote. In 1920, the 19th amendment to the U. S. constitution gave all women the right to vote.

1924/1950s In 1924, the U. S. Congress passed the Indian Citizenship Act, giving U. S. citizenship to all Native Americans. However, it wasn't until the 1950s that Indians were able to vote in all states.

1943/1952 For the first time, in 1943, Chinese-Americans were allowed to become citizens, and to vote. For people from India, citizenship was allowed starting in 1946; for Japanese-Americans and people from other countries in Asia, eligibility for citizenship was finally granted in 1952.

1964 The 24th amendment to the constitution, adopted in 1964, prohibits states from charging a "poll tax" that was mainly intended to exclude African-American voters. A poll tax is a requirement that people pay to vote. (Polls are the places we go to vote.)

1965 The Voting Rights Act was passed by the U. S. Congress, finally ending state practices designed to exclude African-American voters.

1971 The 26th amendment to the U. S. Constitution lowered the voting age from 21 to 18 years.

Agreement about education

But while the writers of the constitution disagreed about many things, there was one area where they all agreed: education. In fact, the most famous part of Washington's constitution is this statement:

"It is the paramount duty of the state to make ample provision for the education of all children residing within its borders, without distinction or preference on account of race, color, caste, or sex."

No other state has such a strong constitutional statement about the importance of public schools. Because this is such a strong statement, courts have ruled that our state legislature has to provide all public schools with enough money to pay for all students' "basic education." It's up to the legislature to define what "basic education" is. (People argue about this often, because what's "basic" changes over time. For instance, computer skills are basic to everyone's education now, but they weren't 25 years ago.)

The result of Washington's definition of education as the state's "paramount duty," is that schools in Washington get most of their funding from the state government. In many other states, schools get most of their funding from local governments.

Also, our constitution says we must educate all children "residing" in Washington – not just those who are citizens. Originally, this was meant to protect (among others) the children of the Chinese immigrants. Today, it makes it clear that immigrants from any country can go to our public schools.

Statehood

The writers of our constitution finished their work, an election was held, and the voters passed the new constitution. Then it was sent off to Washington, D. C. There was just one problem: the governor forgot to sign it. So it had to be sent back to Olympia, signed, and sent back (by train) to the nation's capitol. Finally, on November 11, 1889, Washington became the 42nd state.

The nine separately elected statewide officials in our executive branch are:

Attorney General

Auditor

Commissioner of Public Lands

Governor

Insurance Commissioner

Lieutenant Governor

Secretary of State

Superintendant of Public Instruction

Treasurer

Form No. 1.

THE WESTERN UNION TELEGRAPH COMPANY.

This Company TRANSMITS and DELIVERS messages only on conditions limiting its liability, which have been assented to by the sender of the following message.
Errors can be guarded against only by repeating a message back to the sending station for comparison, and the company will not hold itself liable for errors or delays
in transmission or delivery of Unrepeated Messages, beyond the amount of tolls paid thereon, nor in any case where the claim is not presented in writing within sixty days
after sending the message.
This is an UNREPEATED MESSAGE, and is delivered by request of the sender, under the conditions named above.
THOS. T. ECKERT, General Manager.   NORVIN GREEN, President.

The telegram announcing Washington's statehood was sent collect — which means that the new state governor who received it had to pay for it. This was the federal government's way of saying "OK, you're a grown-up state now, so you have to pay your own bills." At the same time this telegram was sent, another was sent to the outgoing territorial governor, who worked for the federal government – and the federal government paid for that one.

In 1972, Washington voters passed House Joint Resolution (HJR) 61, the Equal Rights Amendment to the state constitution. It had been referred to the voters after having been passed by a 2/3 majority of the state House and Senate.

Amendments

It takes two steps to amend (change) any part of our state constitution. First, both houses of the state legislature have to pass a proposed amendment by a two-thirds majority. Second, the amendment has to be put on the ballot and passed by voters by a simple majority at the next general election. As of 2004, the constitution had been amended 96 times.

One of the most important amendments to the constitution was passed in 1912, when the initiative and referendum were added to the section on the legislative branch of government. (See page 24 for more on this subject.)

In 1972, another amendment was passed to ensure equal rights for women. It reads "Equality of rights and responsibilities under the law shall not be denied or abridged on account of sex." This is called the *equal rights amendment*, or ERA. It was proposed as an amendment to our national constitution, too. But an amendment to our national constitution has to be passed by Congress and ratified (agreed to) by the legislatures of 38 states, and the national ERA never quite achieved that goal. This is an indication of how much more difficult it is to amend our national constitution than our state constitution.

Another interesting amendment was passed in 1988. Our original state constitution said we should have institutions to care for "the blind, deaf, dumb or otherwise defective youth" and the "insane and idiotic." That language was considered normal at the time, but today we think it's mean and insulting. Ralph Munro, who was our Secretary of State for many years, worked to pass a constitutional amendment to change it. He succeeded, and now it reads "youth who are blind or deaf or otherwise disabled"; and "persons who are mentally ill or developmentally disabled."

Washington State Symbols

Nickname:
The Evergreen State

Tree:
Western Hemlock

Flower:
Coast Rhododendron

Grass:
Bluebunch Wheatgrass

Arboretum:
Washington Park Arboretum

Fruit:
Apple

Bird:
Willow Goldfinch

Fish:
Steelhead Trout

Animal:
Roosevelt Elk

Insect:
Common Green Darner Dragonfly

Fossil:
Columbian Mammmoth of North America

Gem:
Petrified Wood

Ship:
"President Washington"

Motto:
"Alki", meaning bye and bye

Song:
"Washington, My Home" by Helen Davis

Folk Song:
"Roll on Columbia, Roll on" by Woodie Guthrie

Dance:
Square Dance

Colors:
Green and Gold

Tartan: (Tartans are special plaid patterns that usually represent a particular family in Scotland.)

The green background represents rich forests; the blue perpendicular bands reflect lakes, rivers and ocean; white is for snow-capped mountains; red for apple and cherry crops; yellow for wheat and grain crops; and black for the eruption of Mount St. Helens

4 A century of change

Economic Change

In 1900, about half a million people were counted in the census in Washington. (A census is a count of how many people live here, conducted by the U. S. government once every ten years.) In the 2000 census, nearly six million people were counted. That's a lot of people – and a lot of change for our state.

photo courtesy Washington State Archives

What we do for a living
based on OFM 2002 data

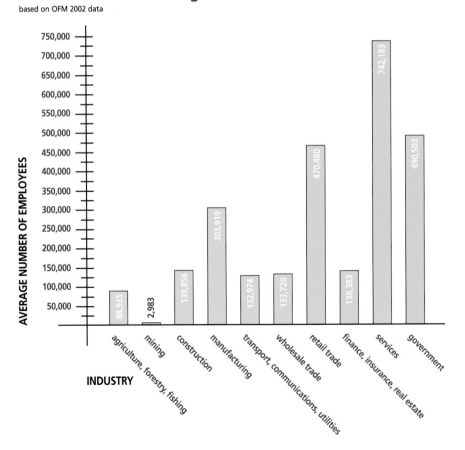

AVERAGE NUMBER OF EMPLOYEES

Industry	Employees
agriculture, forestry, fishing	88,935
mining	2,983
construction	139,856
manufacturing	303,919
transport, communications, utilities	132,974
wholesale trade	133,720
retail trade	470,480
finance, insurance, real estate	138,383
services	742,183
government	490,503

INDUSTRY

Imagine what it was like to live in Washington in the year 1900: People traveled on foot, on horses, on trains, or on boats because cars and airplanes hadn't been invented yet. There was no electricity, so kids did their homework by candle light. Most people only went to school through the 8th grade.

When kids got out of school, many worked on their families' farms. Others got jobs logging forests, milling lumber, mining coal, or working on a fishing boat or in a fish processing plant, or helping to build fast-growing cities and towns. People worked

Who invented the weekend?

At the beginning of the 20th century, people often worked six or even seven days a week, and they often worked for 10 hours a day or more. Even children often worked these long hours. In many jobs, people also suffered a lot of injuries because there were hardly any safety measures.

To win better pay and conditions, workers banded together and formed unions – organizations that represent the interests of workers. Unions tried to bargain with business owners, and to get them to sign contracts spelling out how much workers would be paid, how many hours they would work, and under what conditions.

Sometimes, when the union couldn't get the employer to agree to the pay and conditions they wanted, all the workers would refuse to work. This is called a **strike**.

In 1917, loggers in Washington went on strike because they wanted to reduce their work day from ten hours to eight hours. People who worked in the mills where logs were sawed into lumber joined them, and together, the loggers and mill workers shut down the whole industry. Eventually, they won, and the employers signed contracts giving them an eight-hour day and extra pay if they had to work overtime.

Unions eventually created today's standard work week of 40 hours – eight hours a day, with two days off. Unions also won pensions for people when they get old, paid time off when people are sick, pay for people who are injured at work, health insurance paid by employers, and paid time off for vacations. For many years, the labor movement in Washington was very powerful. But in the last half of the 20th century, the power of unions declined, both in Washington and across the country. Now only about 15% of American workers are union members. Still, unions play a very important part in national, state, and local politics. Unions endorse candidates, and contribute to their campaigns. Many union members work as volunteers to put up signs and pass out literature for the candidates they support, and encourage people to vote.

In recent years, unions have also sponsored successful initiative campaigns to raise the minimum wage, and to provide better pay and union membership for workers who take care of people with disabilities and the elderly.

Washington's changing population

A century and a half ago, Washington's population was almost all Native American. Then the population of white settlers became the overwhelming majority, and Indian tribes dwindled. Over the years, waves of immigrants came from other states and from many countries – mostly European, but some from China, Japan, the Philippines, Mexico and other countries.

Today, Washington's population is still changing and growing. The Hispanic population is growing fastest, and in some counties, Hispanics are or will soon be in the majority. Indian tribes and other populations of people of color are also growing, so that by the end of this century, no single group is likely to comprise a majority of Washington's people.

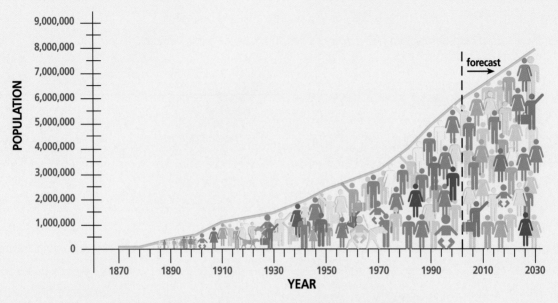

Washington State shows strong historical population growth

The population of Washington State by race/ethnicity

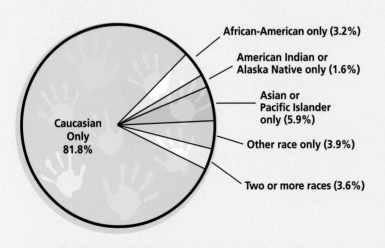

African-American only (3.2%)

American Indian or Alaska Native only (1.6%)

Asian or Pacific Islander only (5.9%)

Other race only (3.9%)

Two or more races (3.6%)

Caucasian Only 81.8%

Washington state population by race
based on US Census Bureau 2000 data

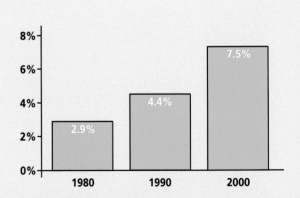

Hispanic population as a percentage of total population

long hours with little time off. And work in the woods, mines, lumber mills and the fishing industry was dangerous. Many workers were hurt or killed in these jobs.

Early in the 20th century, Washington workers began banding together in unions to demand better pay and working conditions. Over many years, unions helped improve the lives of working people by winning the eight-hour day, weekends off, and better safety standards. By the end of the century, however, union membership was going down, and fewer and fewer workers were union members.

By the end of the century, Washington had changed dramatically. The Seattle area had become a center of medical and technical progress – home to a growing biotechnology industry, and famous as the hometown of Bill Gates, the founder of Microsoft. For much of the 20th century, Washington was also known as the place where the Boeing Company built sleek, fast airplanes. In Eastern Washington, technology had transformed the way people farmed, processed food, and managed livestock. But, at the same time, the new importance of technology – and the decline of fishing, mining, and logging – had created a gap between prosperous urban areas and struggling rural communities.

In this new world, even a high school diploma wasn't usually enough to get a good job; the majority of kids went on to college, vocational or technical training, or an apprenticeship. Many adults also went back to school to learn new skills. And young people from rural areas and small towns often had to move to the cities to find good jobs.

The changes of the 20th century brought new prosperity to many, but by the end of the century, there was a growing gap between rich and poor, not just in Washington, but all over the U. S. Rising medical costs were a growing problem – especially for people whose employers didn't pay for their health insurance. And fewer and fewer jobs provided pension benefits for people to live on when they were too old to work anymore.

Change in Washington's natural resources

The 20th century also brought dramatic changes to Washington's natural world. Huge dams were built on our rivers to produce electricity, and to provide irrigation for farms. This made farming a lot more of the land in Eastern Washington possible. But

the Microsoft campus in Redmond

The Department of Natural Resources plants trees after state forests have been cut so that there will be more trees to harvest in 50 or 60 years.

many of these dams blocked salmon from completing their journey from the ocean back to their home streams to lay eggs. The dams also destroyed traditional fishing places that Indians had used for thousands of years.

In the 19th century and in the early years of the 20th century, forests were logged without any thought to the future. At that time, the forests seemed so vast that it was hard to imagine that one day they would all be cut. By the end of the 20th century, scarcely any of Washington's original forests were left. Foresters had learned to replant the areas they cut, but the replanted areas were not the same as the forests that grew there before, because foresters planted only the trees that were most valuable for timber – not all the other plants and trees that had been part of the original forest. Harvesting trees also disrupted many rivers and streams, which did more harm to salmon.

A logger with a felling axe sits in the undercut of a tree in Washington. The tree was 25 feet in diameter.

Even at the beginning of the century, some people began to notice that Washington's industries were damaging fish and streams, and polluting the water and air. Abundant runs of salmon had already started to shrink. But it took a long time for people to face up to these problems. Eventually, laws were passed that required industries to stop dumping wastes into the air and water. But it wasn't until the last decade of the century, when Washington's wild salmon were in danger of extinction, that an all-out effort to save them finally began.

The invention of the automobile also had a profound impact on our natural world. Cars cause a lot of pollution – air pollution from car exhaust, and water pollution from the oil and other fluids that leak from them, and from the materials in tires that wear off on roads and get washed into streams.

The number of wild salmon in our streams has been declining for over a century.

Cars also require a lot of pavement for roads, freeways and parking lots. And where there is pavement, rain can't soak into the ground. Instead, all that rainwater goes somewhere else – it runs into drains, which often gush into lakes or streams, carrying pollutants and disrupting the natural flow of water. The more people move to our state – and the more we drive – the bigger these problems become.

Fishing was a major industry in Washington for much of the 20th century.

The way people lived was part of the problem, too. With every passing decade, people used more electricity and gas, and lived in bigger houses that took more lumber to build. People also created more and more garbage. And there were more and more of us. Urban areas sprawled outward, eating up more land, and needing more parking lots and roads.

This bridge across Lake Washington is filled with bumper-to-bumper traffic during rush hour every day.

Citizens who cared about these problems organized to find solutions, and to urge federal, state, tribal, county and city governments to take action. Starting in the 1960s, these organizations won important victories (including the creation of the state's Department of Ecology) and helped educate people about the problems. Important new laws were passed to reduce the amount of pollution industries could create, and to clean up the most dangerously polluted areas. But governments were hard-pressed to make enough progress to offset continuing population growth, and continuing growth in the number of cars, parking lots, and freeways.

Preserving and restoring the health of the natural world was difficult for other reasons, too. People need jobs, and sometimes this need conflicts with the desire to save wild fish, or preserve forests. Loggers want to cut trees, because their families and communities depend on their income. Fishermen – both Indian and non-Indian – want to fish for the same reason. And governments have to figure out how to pay for cleaning up pollution and saving salmon at a time when they also need to spend more money on schools and colleges, care for the elderly, and other services for six million people.

A second growth forest managed by a forest products company.

Saving Wild Salmon

photo courtesy Washington Department of Fish & Wildlife

For thousands of years salmon have lived in Washington's waters. But now they have disappeared from about half of our rivers and creeks, and wild salmon runs in other rivers and streams are much smaller than they used to be.

There are many reasons why wild salmon are in trouble. Some people blame the problem on too much fishing, but there are other reasons, too. Many of the freshwater rivers and streams where salmon begin and end their lives have been dammed, polluted, or blocked. Some rivers no longer have enough water to support salmon in late summer. And in the winter, floods sometimes destroy salmon eggs or wash young fish out to sea. When it rains, oil from roads, and pesticides from our farms and yards are washed into the streams and rivers.

So many people are worried about salmon that in 1998 the state legislature passed The Salmon Recovery Planning Act. Governor Locke called together the leaders of several state agencies (called the Joint Natural Resources Cabinet) to come up with plans to restore wild salmon. But state government is just one of many partners in this effort. Indian Tribes, the federal government, the governments of other states where salmon live, local governments, and citizens' groups are all involved. Tribal governments are especially important because of their special relationship with salmon, and because the federal court has declared that their treaty rights make them "co-managers" of salmon, on an equal footing with the state. Today tribal, local, state and federal governments all hire a lot of fish biologists and other scientists to help figure out the best ways to restore wild salmon runs.

We can all do something to help. People can volunteer to help restore salmon habitats, and conserve water in farms, factories and homes. We can stop using harmful pesticides and fertilizers on our lawns. We can let our elected officials know what we think they should do. If everyone works together, there is hope for wild salmon.

To learn more go to

www.governor.wa.gov/gsro
The Governor's Salmon Recovery Office

www.wdfw.wa.gov/recovery
The Washington Department of Fish and Wildlife

www.nwifc.wa.gov
The Northwest Indian Fisheries Commission

Change in relationships between tribal and state/local governments

In the 1850s, when the treaties were signed, the U. S. regarded Indian tribes as nations. Treaties are, by definition, agreements between nations. But the tribes were nations within a nation – and they had been defeated by the armed forces of the U. S. government. They didn't have the power to make the federal or state government respect the terms of the treaties. So many of the promises made to Indians in the treaties were soon broken.

In 1887, the U. S. Congress passed the Dawes Act, which said that Indian reservations should be broken up. The federal government assigned each Indian family a plot of land within the reservation, and then sold off some of the remaining land to white settlers. The idea of this policy was to make more land available to white settlers – and to try to make Indians be more like white people. Instead of sharing land, they wanted Indians to adopt the idea of each person or family owning their own land. Instead of hunting, fishing and gathering, they wanted Indians to become farmers. In fact, a lot of people thought Indians should just disappear into the larger society. They didn't think that Indian culture, history, or languages would survive, because there weren't very many Indians left.

Governor Stevens speaking to the Nez Perce, 1855, from the report published with the results of his railroad survey for the Northern Pacific Railroad.

After about forty years, the Dawes Act was reversed, but by then it had already done a lot of damage. Instead of being a single, large tract of land, most reservations had become checkerboards of land owned by Indians and by settlers. Some of the land was eventually returned to the tribes, but most of it was not.

drawing courtesy Governor's Mansion Foundation

During this time, it was nearly impossible for Indians to maintain their traditional forms of government. The federal government basically ran the reservations, through an agency called the Bureau of Indian Affairs (BIA), which is part of the U. S. Department of the Interior. BIA agents ordered Indian children to go to boarding schools – often far away from their home reservations – where they were not allowed to speak their own language. The BIA also had the power to lease Indian lands to mining companies, to dissolve tribal governments, and to decide if and when Indians could sell their land.

In 1934, the U. S. Congress passed the Indian Reorganization Act. This law encouraged the re-formation of tribal governments, and allowed the return of holding land in common for the whole tribe. Many tribes thought this was an important step in the right direction, but there were some problems with the Act. Tribes who chose to form governments under the terms of this legislation were required to adopt tribal constitutions that followed a model set out by the federal government. They also had to agree to govern by majority rule rather than the traditional way of taking time to reach consensus.

In some respects, the tribal constitutions adopted under this law were really designed more for the convenience of the federal government than for the benefit of the tribes. Federal agencies wanted to deal with tribal governments that met federal deadlines – not with traditional tribal practices that meant taking the time to make decisions when the members of a tribe came to an agreement.

In traditional Indian societies, spiritual practices were woven into the way people governed themselves. Spiritual and hereditary leaders were very important. But these traditions were also pushed aside by the new constitutions.

There was another problem, too: to adopt this kind of constitution, and to govern by voting, tribes had to define who was a tribal member. Before settlers came, this wasn't an issue, because people simply participated in the life of the tribe they lived in. People married across tribes, so it was common for kids to have parents from different tribes, or for a husband to participate in the life of his wife's tribe if that was who they lived with. But once tribal government became more structured, people had to formally enroll in one tribe, and one tribe only.

Gathering shellfish on the tidelands

photo courtesy Northwest Indian Fisheries Commission

In 1953, federal policy towards Indians took another terrible turn: the U. S. Congress adopted the "Termination Policy." The aim of this policy was "to make Indians. . . subject to the same laws and entitled to the same privileges and responsibilities as are applicable to other citizens of the United States, (and) to end their status of wards of the United States." To do this, reservations were to be abolished, and tribal governments wiped away. Once again, the federal government wanted Indians to give up their culture, their history, and their identity. This time, they didn't push for Indians to become farmers; instead, they encouraged Indians to move into cities and towns.

The termination policy was reversed in 1970, and in 1975 a new law called the Indian Self-Determination Act was passed. It gave tribes much more power to govern themselves. For the first time, tribes were able to run some of their own health, education, housing, and social services programs, and to make more decisions in tribal courts.

During the 1960s and early 1970s, a long struggle over Indian fishing rights pitted Indians against the Washington state government. State game wardens arrested and fought with Indians who tried to fish in their usual and accustomed places.

In 1974, the U. S. Supreme Court ruled that federal and state governments had to keep the promise in the treaties that said Indians would always be able to fish in common with settlers. Judge George Boldt had ruled that the Indians should get half the salmon harvest; the Supreme Court upheld his decision in 1979.

The Indian Self-Determination Act and the Boldt decision were important turning points. The federal government finally recognized that Indians were not going to disappear, and that in spite of everything that had happened to them, Indians retained their own cultures, history, and identity. Indian tribes – and their governments – are a permanent part of the United States. The treaties that the U. S. government signed with tribes are the law of the land.

Since the 1970s, both the federal and state governments have begun to create "government to government" relationships with tribes. This is a return to the idea, embodied in the treaties, that Indian tribes are nations within a nation – that they have a right to govern themselves as they choose, and to protect and preserve their culture and traditions.

photo courtesy Debbie Preston, Northwest Indian Fisheries Commission

The changing challenges of government

As you can imagine, all the changes of the 20th century had a big impact on our governments – state, tribal, and local – not to mention our national government. These changes are reflected in the speech Governor Gary Locke gave to the opening session of the state legislature in 1999:

> " One hundred years ago, in the final days of the 19th century, Governor John Rogers stood before the legislature and delivered the state of the state address. Governor Rogers was a former state legislator, and the prime sponsor of the "Barefoot Schoolboy Act," which established state funding for public schools. At that time, public schooling meant an 8th grade education for most children.
>
> In his 1899 speech, Governor Rogers called for something very controversial: extending public education from the 8th grade to the 12th grade! He also asked the legislature to fund circulating libraries in horse-drawn wagons, because he believed that if students developed a taste for good reading "a vast and incalculable good (would) be done, and the character of the future men and women of this state (would) be elevated to a higher plane."
>
> Today, as we stand on the cusp of another new century, it is vital that we reflect on what we have gained, and what we have learned in the last hundred years.
>
> At the time of Governor Rogers' 1899 speech, the population of Washington was 500,000. And when he addressed the legislature, he faced an all-male group. Women in Washington State were still 11 years away from winning the vote.
>
> Today, our state's population is over five and one-half million, and still growing. And Washington holds the proud distinction of having the highest percentage of female legislators in the United States.
>
> When Governor Rogers held office, industries freely dumped vast amounts of raw waste into our rivers and bays. Children as young as 10 years old worked in factories. And in most industries, people worked long hours, in dangerous conditions, and were without the most basic workers' rights.
>
> Clearly, we have made progress in this century. But now we must chart our course for the next century.
>
> None of us can predict what our world will be like a hundred years from now. We know that our population will continue to grow and become more diverse,

Burbank Country School, 1901

photo courtesy Washington State Historical Society, Tacoma

our technology and economy will be transformed, and scientific advances will continue to astonish us. Dramatic progress in medicine and health care will mean that many – perhaps even most – of the children born this year – like (my daughter) Emily's little brother or sister – will actually live to see the beginning of the 22nd century.

But although we can see only the dimmest outline of what lies ahead, three things are imperative:

First, to succeed in the coming century, education must become a larger part of all our lives – and education of our children must become an even higher priority.

Second, we must learn to live in harmony with the natural world that sustains us, and we must protect the wild salmon, the rivers, the forests and the agricultural lands that will sustain the people of the 21st century and beyond.

And third, we must learn to live in harmony with each other. We must learn to be more civil, more respectful of our differences, and more appreciative of our diversity. 〞

Education in 2002

photo courtesy of Gayle Rieber Photography

As you can see, the challenge of governing the state changed a lot in 100 years. During the 20th century, our state went from being a remote, wild place to being a leader in technology, agriculture, and international trade. Our governments grew and changed along with our population. There was more for governments to do – and more costs for taxpayers to pay. At the beginning of the century, we only had to pay for educating a few thousand kids through the 8th grade. Only a few of these students ever went to college. By the end of the century, government needed money to pay for schools for nearly a million students in kindergarten through high school – and about half of them went on to community and technical colleges or four-year universities. By the end of the century, we also needed more roads, more money for health care, more services for people with disabilities and the elderly, and more jails, police and firefighters.

At the beginning of the century, Washington state government's annual budget was about $30 million in today's dollars; by the end of the century, it was about $11 **billion** a year.

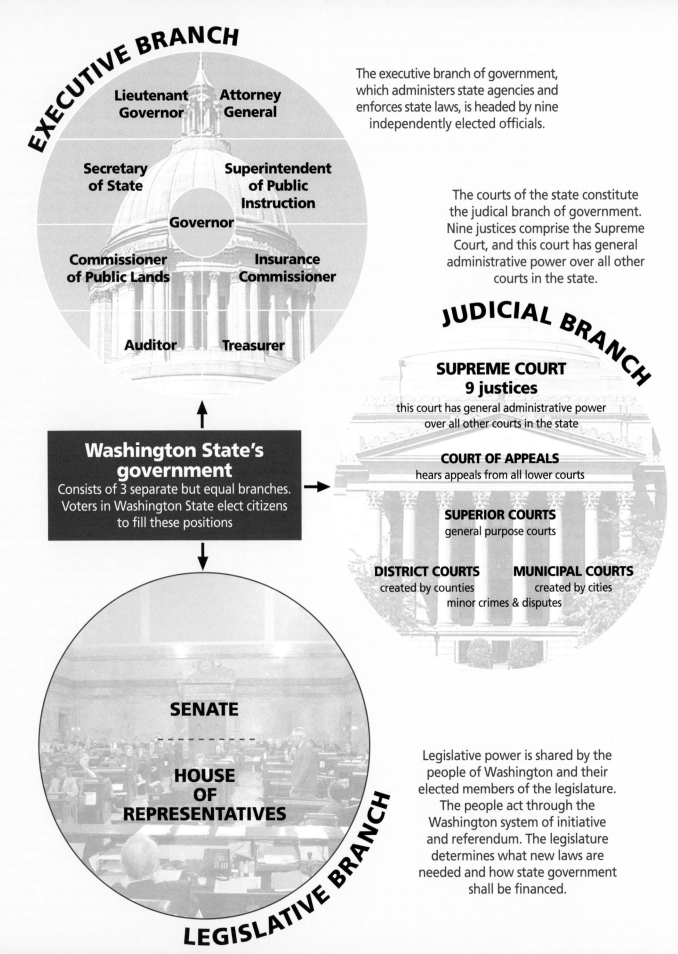

EXECUTIVE BRANCH

Lieutenant Governor

Attorney General

Secretary of State

Superintendent of Public Instruction

Governor

Commissioner of Public Lands

Insurance Commissioner

Auditor

Treasurer

The executive branch of government, which administers state agencies and enforces state laws, is headed by nine independently elected officials.

The courts of the state constitute the judicial branch of government. Nine justices comprise the Supreme Court, and this court has general administrative power over all other courts in the state.

JUDICIAL BRANCH

SUPREME COURT
9 justices
this court has general administrative power over all other courts in the state

COURT OF APPEALS
hears appeals from all lower courts

SUPERIOR COURTS
general purpose courts

DISTRICT COURTS
created by counties

MUNICIPAL COURTS
created by cities
minor crimes & disputes

Washington State's government

Consists of 3 separate but equal branches. Voters in Washington State elect citizens to fill these positions

SENATE

- - - - - - - - -

HOUSE OF REPRESENTATIVES

Legislative power is shared by the people of Washington and their elected members of the legislature. The people act through the Washington system of initiative and referendum. The legislature determines what new laws are needed and how state government shall be financed.

LEGISLATIVE BRANCH

5 Governing Washington today

Governing Washington today may be more complicated than it was a hundred years ago, but the basic structure of our government is still the same. Our form of government has been flexible enough to change with the times, and stable enough to prevent change from being too sudden or extreme. That's mainly because our national and state constitutions have provided a strong foundation that has stood the test of time. The basic ideas in our constitutions – regular democratic elections, separation of powers, the rule of law, and clearly defined rights and responsibilities for citizens – have become deeply ingrained in our way of life.

The founding principles and practices in both our state and national constitutions are reflected in today's state government.

The legislature

The legislature has two halves – the House of Representatives, and the Senate.

Our national government's legislative branch is organized the same way, so sometimes people get confused about which Senate is the U. S. Senate, and which one is the *state* Senate. There's a big difference!

The U. S. Senate and the U. S. House of Representatives make laws for the whole United States, but our state Senate and House of Representatives make laws only *for the state of Washington.*

The people of this state do not yield their sovereignty to the agencies which serve them. The people, in delegating authority, do not give their public servants the right to decide what is good for the people to know and what is not good for them to know. The people insist on remaining informed so that they may retain control over the instruments they have created.

RCW 42.30.010, A PORTION OF THE LAW KNOWN AS THE "OPEN MEETINGS ACT," PASSED BY THE LEGISLATURE IN 1971.

Our state is divided into 49 legislative districts. The people in each of these districts elect one state Senator and two state Representatives. State senators serve for four years terms, but Representatives are elected every two years.

Making the Laws

The state legislature meets every year beginning in January. Every other year, they must agree on a two-year state budget. This two-year period is called a *biennium*. In the year when they must agree on a biennial budget, the legislative session lasts longer –usually 105 days. In the second year of the biennium, the legislative session is shorter, and usually ends after 60 days. Sometimes legislators don't finish their work in this amount of time. When this happens – or when an important issue comes up at other times of the year – they have "special sessions" that can last anywhere from one to 30 days.

Both the House and the Senate divide up into committees, and each committee studies proposals to change the laws in a specific area. There are Senate and House committees on public schools, transportation, health and human services, agriculture, local government, energy, trade and economic development, the environment, and other topics.

Kids as legislators, trial lawyers, and legislative staff

If you want to know what it's like to be a state legislator, the YMCA Youth and Government program is just for you. Students meet for several months to learn how to research and develop legislation, and then hold a four-day mock legislative session in Olympia. Each student assumes the role of a House member, a Senator, or a state elected official such as Governor or Secretary of State.

The YMCA also has a program for kids who are interested in the law. Teams of students prepare a mock case for trial, and act as attorneys and witnesses. A real judge, in a real courtroom, hears their case, and a "jury" of real attorneys rates teams for their presentation.

If you're interested in either of these programs, contact your local YMCA.
Another way for students to learn about the legislature is to apply to be a page. A page is a student (age 14-17) who works for the Senate or House of Representatives in Olympia for one week during a legislative session. Pages deliver messages and do other duties, and also participate in special classes where they learn how the legislature works. If you're interested in applying to be a page, contact one of your two House members or your Senator.

photo by Ron Soliman, May 8, 2004, reprinted courtesy *The Olympian*

Legislative Districts in Washington state

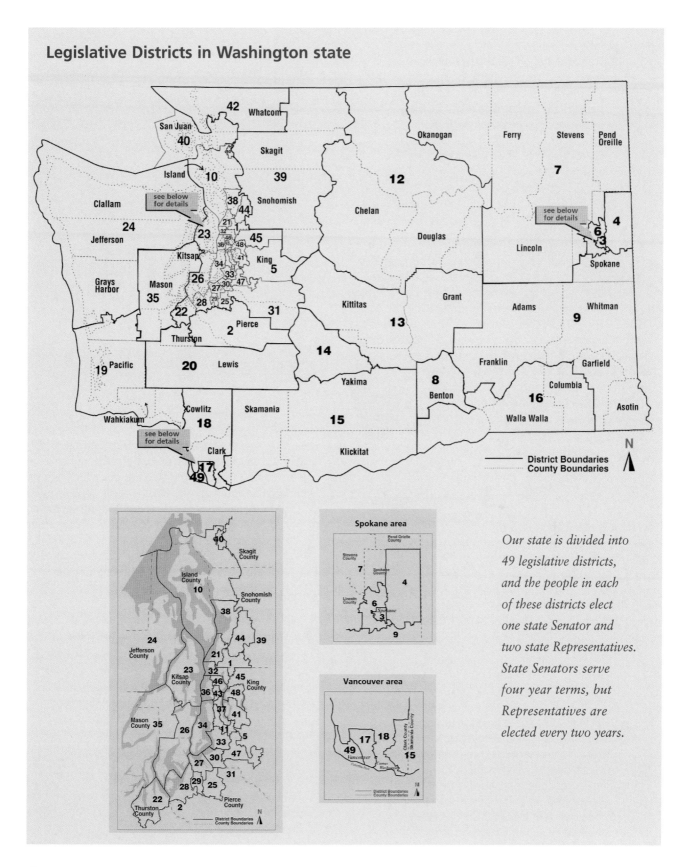

Our state is divided into 49 legislative districts, and the people in each of these districts elect one state Senator and two state Representatives. State Senators serve four year terms, but Representatives are elected every two years.

How an idea becomes a law:

1 Someone has an idea – they think a new law should be made, or an existing law should be changed. The person who has the idea might be the governor or some other elected official, or it might be a business or union leader or any other ordinary citizen.

2 The legislator who is going to introduce the proposed law or change (called a bill) asks someone on their staff to write a first draft. Usually, the draft is reviewed by the people who asked the state legislator to introduce it. Sometimes other people who have an interest in the topic are asked to review it, too, and to say whether they think it can get enough votes to pass. A bill may be revised many times before it is ever introduced.

HOUSE ⟷ SENATE

3 Once a bill is drafted, it goes to the Code Reviser's office, where people who are experts on Washington law go over it. They make sure it is technically correct, and decide where it would fit in to the Revised Code of Washington — the body of laws of our state.

6 Even bills that pass out of committee don't always get voted on by the full House or Senate. The Rules Committee decides which bills will be voted on, and when. At this stage, legislative leaders may decide to hold off on voting on a bill while people try to resolve any arguments they have about it. They rarely bring a bill up for a vote until they know that enough people agree on it for it to pass the full House or Senate.

7 Finally, a bill that has cleared all these hurdles comes up for a vote in the full House or Senate. If it passes, then it starts the whole process over again in the opposite house. Once again, it is introduced, referred to a committee, discussed in committee, referred back to the Rules Committee and then to the full House or Senate. It can be amended along the way. If the House and Senate pass versions of the bill that aren't exactly the same, they have to work out the differences and pass the bill over again.

4 The legislator who is going to introduce the bill may pass it around to other legislators to see if they want to be co-sponsors. Then the bill is introduced in either the House or the Senate, and referred to a committee. For instance, all bills that will affect public schools are sent to the Education Committee; all bills dealing with roads go to the Transportation Committee, and so forth.

photo of the capitol building courtesy of Washington State Department of General Administration; photos 5, 7, & 8 courtesy of Washington State Senate Photo

5

The committee chair decides whether the committee will consider the bill. If the chair chooses to, he or she schedules a public hearing on the bill. A public hearing is a meeting where anyone can come and tell the committee what they think about the bill. Then the committee discusses it. They may decide to amend (or change) it. Then they vote to either send it to the full House or Senate for a vote, or to kill it.

or   BILL

8

When a bill has passed both the House and Senate, it goes to the Governor. The Governor can sign it into law, or veto it. If the Governor vetoes it, both the House and the Senate can override the veto if they pass the bill by a two-thirds majority. When the Governor signs a bill into law, there is almost always a special ceremony. The Governor invites the people who worked to pass the law to his office. They all have their picture taken together, and the Governor gives one of them the pen that he or she uses to sign it.

When a legislator wants to write a new law or change an existing law, he or she introduces a bill that spells out what should be changed. First the bill is sent to a committee, where committee members study it. The committees hold public hearings on bills so that citizens and lobbyists can say what they think about it. The committee may also change the bill. This is called *amending* it. If the bill will cost money, it goes to a special committee that writes the budget. Then the bill goes to the full House or Senate. If the House votes to pass the bill, then it goes to the Senate; when the Senate passes a bill, then it goes to the House. Bills can be amended in the full House and Senate, too.

As you can imagine, it's not easy to get a bill passed through this long and complicated process. And even when legislators do get a bill passed, they still have to persuade the governor to sign it before it can become law.

Both the Senate and the House have to pass a bill with exactly the same wording before it can become law. If they have different versions of the same bill, they have to work out the differences, and then vote on it again.

After both the House and the Senate pass a bill, it goes to the Governor. He or she can either sign the bill into law, or veto it. (There's more about this in a few pages, when we get to the section on the Executive Branch.)

As you can imagine, it's not easy to get a bill passed through this long and complicated process. And even when legislators do get a bill passed, they still have to persuade the governor to sign it before it can become law. In fact, this system is purposely designed to make it pretty difficult to pass a new law, because it's important for people to take their time and think carefully about the laws they are making. It's also important for the public to have time to hear about bills, and tell their legislators how they want them to vote.

In spite of this complicated system, hundreds of bills pass and become law during every legislative session — and most of them pass with bipartisan support. In spite of the strong role of political parties, there are a lot of bills that people in both parties agree on.

We pay taxes to the federal government, to state government, and to our local governments.

The charts on this page show where our STATE government gets its money, and how the money is spent.

The chart on the left shows that just over half of the money to run state government comes from taxes we pay to the state.

In the same chart, you can also see that just over 25% of our state budget is actually money from the taxes we pay to the federal government. The federal government sends some of our tax dollars back to state and local governments for certain purposes. The federal government sends this money with "strings attached," which means that the state has to abide by federal rules about how the money is spent. In some cases, the state has to "match" the federal money. For instance, in the Medicaid program (which pays for health care for low-income people), the federal government pays about half the cost, and the state pays the other half.

In the chart on the right, you can see why people say that most of the state budget is spent to "educate, medicate, and incarcerate" people. (Incarcerate means put in prison or jail.) The biggest part of the budget is spent on public schools, colleges and universities. Most of the spending on "social and health services" is for medical care for low-income people.

Where state government gets its money

(from the proposed 2003-2005 budget)

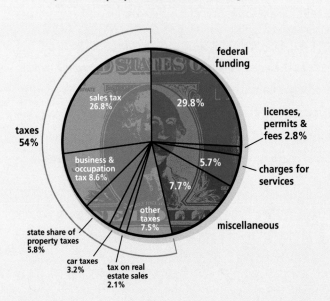

- taxes 54%
- sales tax 26.8%
- federal funding 29.8%
- licenses, permits & fees 2.8%
- business & occupation tax 8.6%
- charges for services 5.7%
- other taxes 7.5%
- miscellaneous 7.7%
- state share of property taxes 5.8%
- car taxes 3.2%
- tax on real estate sales 2.1%

How the state spends its money

(from the proposed 2003-2005 budget, state funds only)

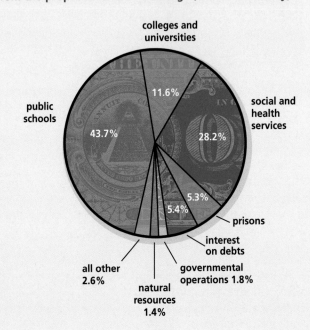

- colleges and universities 11.6%
- public schools 43.7%
- social and health services 28.2%
- prisons 5.3%
- interest on debts 5.4%
- governmental operations 1.8%
- natural resources 1.4%
- all other 2.6%

The legislature's biggest job: the state budget and taxes

Today the state's general fund budget is about $11 billion a year. By anyone's measure, that's a lot of money. And that's just the *operating budget* – the money that's spent to keep schools, colleges, and other government services operating. There is also a *capital budget* for building new buildings, and a separate *transportation budget* for highways, bridges, public transit and ferries.

All that money comes from taxes and fees paid by people who live, work, and shop in Washington. When we buy things, we pay sales tax. If we own property, we pay property taxes. Businesses also pay various kinds of taxes.

Every two years, there are lively debates about how much to spend for public schools, colleges and universities, social and health services, and protection of the environment, among other things.

A lively debate

In the early 1990s, health care costs were rising fast. Every year, health care took a bigger bite out of the state budget, because the state provides health benefits to state employees, and pays about half the cost of health care for people on Medicaid, which is a health insurance program for people who have very low incomes. (The federal government pays the other half.) Because costs were rising so fast, more and more people couldn't afford health insurance, but weren't poor enough to qualify for Medicaid. It was a huge problem.

There was a long and very lively debate in the legislature about what to do. Some people thought that all employers should be required to provide health insurance for their employees. Some thought the state should collect more taxes, and provide everyone with health insurance. Others thought that only the federal government could solve this problem. And some thought that health care should be an individual responsibility, and that government should stay out of it.

After many public hearings, commissions, reports, and debates, the legislature finally passed a health care reform law in 1993. But parts of the law were found to violate federal rules, and other parts were later repealed by the legislature.

Now the debate about health care is heating up again, because costs are rising fast, and there are still a lot of people whose employers don't provide health insurance.

photo courtesy of Swedish Medical Center

There are equally lively debates about whether to raise or lower taxes, and whether to change the kinds of taxes that people and businesses pay.

The Role of Political Parties

Political parties have a lot to do with how the legislature works. In both the House and the Senate, the political party that has the most members – the majority party – has a lot more power. The majority party's leaders choose who will chair each of the committees. Committee chairs are almost always members of the majority party. This is important because the committee chair decides which bills the committee will study and vote on. If the committee chair doesn't like a bill, he or she can simply decide not to bring it up in committee.

The majority party also gets to choose who will be the chair for meetings of the full House or Senate. In the House, the person in charge is called the *Speaker of the House.* The Senate is a little bit different: the Lieutenant Governor is the *presiding officer* of the Senate, and leads the Senate through the process of voting on bills. But the *Senate Majority Leader* – the leader of the majority party – is the most powerful person in the Senate, because he or she (along with other top leaders of his or her political party) controls who is assigned to chair and sit on committees, and what bills will come up for a vote.

In both the House and the Senate, political parties have *caucuses* – that is, all the Representatives or Senators of one party meet to discuss specific issues or bills, and to decide how to vote on them. No one else is allowed to come to these meetings.

Usually, members of one party stick together, because they have more power when they do, and because they share the same philosophy about what government should do. But sometimes there are strong disagreements within a political party, and occasionally legislators vote with the opposite party. Most of the

Bipartisan: *supported by members of two political parties; in our case, this means supported by both Republicans and Democrats. ("Bi" means two; "partisan" means someone who supports a particular cause or political party.) So "a bipartisan solution" would be one supported by both Republicans and Democrats.*

Who owns the water?

Grand Coulee Dam

Nothing is more basic to all life than water. Without it, we would die in just a few days. But as our population grows – and as our farms, ranches, and orchards grow – the demand for water has become a big problem.

In every state legislative session for the past fifteen years, there have been debates about water. Some people want more water to irrigate their farms and orchards. Others want more water for cities and towns. And some people want to leave more water in streams and rivers to help salmon and other fish survive.

Over two-thirds of the electricity we use comes from the dams that have been built across our rivers. Some of the dams were originally built to provide water for irrigation. These dams made a lot of the agriculture in Eastern Washington possible. Today, their role as producers of electricity is also vital. However, some dams – like the Grand Coulee Dam – block the passage of fish from their spawning grounds to the sea.

The dams also ruined many traditional Indian fishing places.

It is extremely difficult to settle conflicts over water. The state grants water rights – the right to drill wells or take water from a river. The state has to be careful not to grant too many water rights, or the rivers and wells will run dry. But people get very angry if they have to wait a long time for a permit to drill a well, or if they are told they can't.

The federal government built many of the dams, so it is involved in the debates about water, too. Indian tribes also have important legal rights to water on reservations. And federal laws to protect wild salmon say that we have to have enough cold, clean water in the rivers and streams to protect salmon from dying out.

There just aren't any easy answers to these conflicts. As our state's population grows, these disputes will become even more difficult. Federal, tribal, state and local governments will all have to work together to find solutions, and even then, no one is likely to be fully satisfied.

A wheat farmer

time, this is not a big problem. But sometimes, when the issue is important and the vote is close, people get very upset about a legislator not voting with their caucus. When this happens, the caucus leader may find a way to punish the person who strays from the party position. For instance, that person might not get the committee assignments they want, or a bill they want passed might not be brought up for a vote.

Legislative Staff

As Washington has grown, the number of people who work for the state legislature has grown, too. Both the House and the Senate have experts to advise them about the complicated state budget, and about issues such as the environment, transportation, and education. Part of the staff is non-partisan; that is, these staff people are not allied with either political party, and they work for all the legislators. But the party caucuses in the Senate and the House also have their own, partisan staff that is loyal to the caucus they work for.

Washington's capitol building in Olympia was the last state capitol building to be built with a rotunda, a round building with a dome.

photo courtesy Leslie Hoge Design

Teen Driving Restrictions Save Lives

Fatal traffic collisions involving teenage drivers are the leading cause of death for people between the ages of 15 and 20. To reduce this risk, the Washington legislature passed a law in 1999 that restricts teen driving. The law says that for the first six months after a teen gets a driver's license, he

or she can't have any passengers under age 20 in the car unless they are family members. After six months, drivers under the age of 18 are allowed to have three passengers under the age of 20 who are not family members. Teens under 18 are also not allowed to drive between 1 AM and 5 AM

unless they are with a licensed driver who is 25 or older, or unless they have to drive very early in the morning because they work on a farm, orchard or ranch.

After one year of driving – with no tickets or accidents – these restrictions are dropped. But if drivers under the age of 18 get two traffic tickets, their license is suspended for six months, and if they get a

third ticket, they lose their license until they turn 18.

A similar law passed in Florida in 1995 reduced the number of deaths and injuries caused by teen drivers. By 2004, 33 states had adopted laws like this.

For more information about this, take a look at the Teen Page of the state Department of Licensing web site at: http://www.dol.wa.gov/ds/teen.htm.

People from all walks of life and professions become state legislators. *Here are just a few of the jobs and professions held by state legislators:*

Members of the House of Representatives:

Tom Campbell,
a Republican from Pierce County, is a chiropractor. He also owns a small farm, and used to be a Captain in the Army Special Forces.

Eileen Cody,
a Democrat from West Seattle, is a registered nurse.

John Lovick,
a Democrat from Snohomish County, is a state patrol officer.

John McCoy,
a Democrat, is a member of the Tulalip tribe. He works with computers, and once held a job as a computer technician in the White House in Washington, D. C.

Dan Newhouse,
a Republican from Sunnyside, is a farmer.

Senators:

Joyce Mullikan,
a Republican from Ephrata, worked as a classroom interpreter for the deaf.

Rosa Franklin,
a Democrat from Tacoma, is a registered nurse who specializes in women's health care.

Mark Doumit,
a Democrat from Cathlamet, owns a tree farm and is a commercial fisherman.

Linda Evans Parlette,
a Republican from Wenatchee, has an orchard and is a pharmacist

Immigrants who become U. S. citizens can also become state legislators.

Velma Veloria,
a member of the House of Representatives, is originally from the Philippines, and now lives in Seattle.

Senator Paull Shin
is originally from South Korea, and now lives in Snohomish County.

The public's right to know

Disclosure: *to reveal or expose something that was unknown or secret; for instance you could disclose what's in a box by taking the lid off. In discussions about government, when people talk about "public disclosure" they are talking about making sure the public can see what's going on, rather than having things hidden from view. The term "transparency" is used to mean the same thing. ("Transparent" means you can see through something; a window, for instance, is transparent.)*

Washington's Public Disclosure Commission

In 1972, the Coalition for Open Government wrote an initiative to let the public in on some secrets – namely, where politicians and lobbyists got their money, and how they spent it. The initiative required all candidates for office to report where their personal income came from, and who gave how much to their campaigns. It also required lobbyists to report where they got their money, how much they spent, and what they spent it on. The initiative passed.

In 1973, the initiative resulted in the creation of the state Public Disclosure Commission. Now candidates for office and lobbyists have to file reports so the public can see who's supporting whom, and who's lobbying for what. You can read their reports on the PDC web site at **www.pdc.wa.gov.**

There are also many staff people who work to manage the vast amount of paperwork it takes to get bills through the legislature. Publishing all the schedules of committee meetings, distributing copies of all the bills that are introduced, and keeping records of everything that happens is a lot of work.

The part-time legislature

Being a state Senator or Representative is a part-time job, because the legislature usually meets for only two or three months a year. Most of our state legislators have regular jobs, or run their own farms or businesses, and take time off to go to Olympia for the two or three months when the legislature is in session.

The people who wrote our state constitution wanted it this way, because they thought people who worked at regular jobs would make better laws — laws that really served the needs of ordinary people like themselves. They didn't want to create a separate profession of politicians; they wanted the legislature to really be "of the people, by the people, and for the people."

It's getting harder, though, for state legislators to keep their regular jobs while they are serving in the legislature. Over time, as the state's population has grown and our society has become more complex, the work of making laws for the state has grown, too. It takes more and more of legislators' time to attend longer sessions of the legislature, to go to committee meetings that are held in between sessions, and to learn all they need to know about complicated issues. It also takes time to run campaigns so that they can get elected or re-elected.

Legislators are paid about $30,000 a year – and they get extra money for living expenses when they must travel to special meetings and to regular legislative sessions. Some legislators live on this amount of money. Some have other income from savings or an inheritance. And some have spouses with full time jobs, so they don't have to have another job.

How state legislators are elected

Ordinary people can run for and get elected to the state legislature. Since there are only about 120,000 people in a legislative district, campaigns for the legislature are pretty low-budget, local affairs. The main ways candidates try to get people to vote for them are:

Doorbelling – this means the candidate walks up to people's houses or apartments, rings their doorbell, and tries to chat with residents about why they should vote for the candidate. Sometimes candidates get their friends to doorbell for them, too.

Candidate forums are public meetings where all the candidates for office are invited to give speeches about why they are running for office, and to answer questions from the audience.

Yard signs are used to make sure everyone knows the candidate's name, and to show that a lot of people are supporting them.

News coverage in local newspapers, and sometimes on radio or TV stations, helps candidates become better known to voters.

You can watch!

TVW is a television network that broadcasts many state government events. On TVW, you can watch lawyers present cases to the state Supreme Court, observe the legislature debate issues and pass new laws, and see press conferences with the Governor and other state officials. TVW also has a web site (http://tvw.org/) where you can find past events and listen to them or watch them on your computer.
You can look at the TV listings in your local newspaper to find out what channel TVW is on in your community.

High standards for our students and schools

photo courtesy Leslie Hoge Design

In the 1980s, people worried that students in public schools weren't learning enough. Many high school graduates had drifted through school without really studying. A high school diploma just didn't mean very much, because many graduates really didn't have the reading, writing, or math skills they needed to get good jobs or to be good citizens.

In 1993, after several years of debate, the legislature passed a major school reform act that sets academic standards that all students will have to meet in order to graduate from high school. It is taking a long time to put this in practice, though. First, committees of teachers, parents and business people had to decide what the standards would be for each subject area. Then experts developed the tests (called the Washington Assessments of Student Learning, or WASLs) to measure whether students were meeting the standards. Over several years, teachers were trained in teaching to the new standards. Because this is so important, no one wanted to rush through this process. Right now, students who graduate in 2008 are scheduled to be the first who will have to pass the 10th grade WASL to graduate. Now people are worried about what will happen if a lot of students can't pass the test. In 2004, the legislature passed a new law that gives all students the opportunity to retake the tests if they don't pass the first time.

Fundraisers are like parties; the host invites a lot of people, and provides snacks and drinks. The candidate comes and "works the room," that is, he or she goes around meeting people, shaking their hands, and chatting with as many of them as possible. Then the candidate gives a little speech about why she is running for office, and what she intends to do if she is elected. Finally, the host asks everyone to contribute to the candidate's election campaign fund, work on their campaign, and to vote for them.

Mailings of brochures about the candidate are sent – usually only to registered voters – in the candidate's district. In many campaigns, writing, designing, printing and mailing these brochures is the most expensive part of the campaign.

Endorsements are like sponsorships from unions, business associations, or advocacy groups like environmental or civil rights organizations. When an organization endorses a candidate, they urge all their members to vote for that person, and they usually contribute money to the candidate's campaign.

Paid political advertising in newspapers, or on radio or TV, is becoming a larger and larger part of legislative campaigns. Because it is so much more expensive than any of the other ways people campaign, it is driving up the cost of running for the legislature.

People complain that these campaigns are getting more expensive to run, but compared to statewide or national political campaigns, they will always be small potatoes. Running for the state legislature is still within the reach of any ordinary citizen who has a reputation for caring about their community, and enough friends and supporters to help them run a good campaign. Often, people don't get elected the first time they run, but if they keep trying, and more people get to know them, they succeed on their second or third try.

The YMCA Youth in Government program

Most (but not all) of the people who run for the legislature have some previous experience in government. They may have served on a local city council, or been active in local school committees or other candidates' political campaigns.

Usually, people get elected to the House of Representatives first, and then run for a state Senate seat a few years later, when they are more experienced. Moving from the House to the Senate is considered a promotion because there are twice as many members in the House of Representatives as there are in the Senate. (One Senator per legislative district = 49 Senators; two Representatives per legislative district = 98 members of the

photo by Ron Soliman, May 8, 2004, reprinted courtesy *The Olympian*

House of Representatives.) In the Senate, where there are only half as many voting members, each vote carries more weight. People also prefer to serve in the Senate because Senators only have to run for re-election every four years rather than every two years.

Chapter 5 Governing Washington today

page 67

Many state legislators also go on to run for local offices that are full-time jobs, such as county commissioner or (in bigger cities) city council members. Others run for higher offices such as Governor, Lands Commissioner, State Supreme Court Justice, or U. S. Representative or Senator.

The Executive Branch

Washington's executive branch is different from many other states. In most states, the governor is one of three or four state elected officials, so he or she has a lot of power. In Washington, the governor is one of nine statewide elected officials. (The reason for this is explained in the section on the state constitution in Chapter 3.)

But while Washington's governor may have less power than governors in most other states, our governor still has a lot to do. The governor writes the first draft of the state budget, and sends it to the legislature. The governor has a big influence on the legislature, because he or she can veto bills or parts of bills, including the state budget. The governor also gets his or her allies in the legislature to introduce bills that he or she wants to become law.

But the governor's biggest job is running state government. The governor hires and is the boss of the directors of 40 state agencies. These agencies run state prisons and mental hospitals; provide health care and other services to low-income people, the elderly, and people with disabilities; license cars, drivers, businesses and professions; and protect the environment.

There are another 88 agencies that are governed by boards or commissions (groups of specially selected people that oversee the agency), and the governor appoints some or all of the members of these groups. The governor also chooses the boards of trustees that govern state colleges and universities. It takes two or three people working full time in the Governor's office just to recruit and screen people for all these positions, and to advise the Governor on these appointments.

The governor also works with the U. S. government on many issues. If there is a flood or other disaster, the governor asks the federal government for emergency assistance. If there are issues before the U. S. congress that will affect our state, the governor meets with our state's congressional representatives to make sure our state's

The Department of Licensing

About 1,200 people work at the Department of Licensing. In offices all over the state, they license drivers, cars, trucks and boats. They also license businesses, and hundreds of professions ranging from accountants to manicurists to wrestlers. And they license facilities such as drug treatment centers, migrant labor camps, and shelters for victims of domestic violence. The fees for these licenses help pay for government services.

Licensing is an important way for government to make sure that citizens are protected. The Department of Licensing requires that people get proper training and pass a test before they get a license to drive a car or truck, provide services to the public, or open a facility like a child care center.

The Department of Social and Health Services (DSHS)

DSHS is the biggest state agency; it has 18,000 employees in offices all over the state. It is responsible for helping people in need of emergency help or health care, making sure that people with disabilities and the elderly get the services they need, protecting children from abuse and neglect, and taking care of the state's most difficult juvenile delinquents.

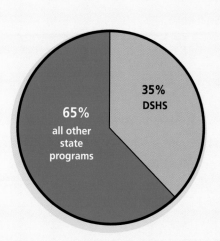

35% DSHS

65% all other state programs

DSHS's share of state budget

In this pie chart, the DSHS budget looks like a larger share of the state budget than in the chart on page 58. That's because this pie chart includes funds that the federal government sends to our state, and the other one includes only state funds.

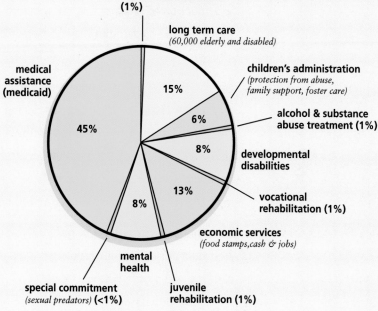

central administration (1%)

long term care
(60,000 elderly and disabled)

15%

children's administration
(protection from abuse, family support, foster care)

6%

alcohol & substance abuse treatment (1%)

8%

developmental disabilities

medical assistance (medicaid)

45%

vocational rehabilitation (1%)

13%

economic services
(food stamps,cash & jobs)

8%

juvenile rehabilitation (1%)

mental health

special commitment
(sexual predators) **(<1%)**

How DSHS's share of budget is spent

The Asian Pacific American Affairs Commission

The Asian Pacific American Affairs Commission is one of several small agencies that advocate for the rights of people of color in Washington. Three staff people work for this Commission. The 12 Commissioners are appointed by the Governor to serve three-year terms. The Commissioners are from all over the state. They don't get paid for being on the Commission, although the state pays their expenses when they travel to a meeting. The purpose of the Commission is to advocate for

the interests of Asian Pacific Americans in Washington, and to advise the governor, the legislature, and state agencies about their needs.

The other agencies that represent people of color are the African-American Affairs Commission, the Hispanic Affairs Commission, and the Governor's Office of Indian Affairs.

A list of all state government agencies is available on the state government web site at www.access.wa.gov.

needs are known. The governor is also a member of the National Governors' Association, which meets once each year with the U. S. president to talk about relations between state governments and our national government.

The governor can convene special commissions to study issues and make recommendations for changes. In the last few years, groups called together by the governor have issued reports on how to improve the state's business climate, how to protect people with disabilities from abuse, how to improve the state's colleges and universities, and how to reform the state's tax structure. The recommendations of these groups aren't always enacted, but they do have a lot of influence.

One of the governor's most important roles is to provide leadership to the people of the state. The governor does this in many ways. Each year, the governor gives a "state of the state" speech at the beginning of the legislative session that helps everyone focus on what important issues need to be addressed. And throughout the year, the governor gives speeches to business and community groups all over the state, and listens to people's concerns and problems. The governor encourages people to be active citizens, to volunteer in their communities, and to help make our state a better place.

The governor and his or her family also become a symbol of our state. States that elect goofy or corrupt governors get a reputation for being goofy or corrupt. States that elect respected governors get respect.

The other executive branch officials that we elect are:

The Lieutenant Governor presides over sessions of the state Senate. Legally, the Lieutenant Governor is the Governor when the Governor is out of state, but in practice, the governor's staff takes care of things when he or she is away. The lieutenant governor really only has a part-time job, since the Senate is usually in session for only two or three months a year. But the Lieutenant Governor gets a full-time salary, and can use his time to do whatever he thinks is important. Our current Lieutenant Governor uses his time to discourage drug and alcohol abuse, and to promote international trade.

The Secretary of State supervises state and local elections, and certifies the results of state primaries and general elections. (County officials, however, register people to

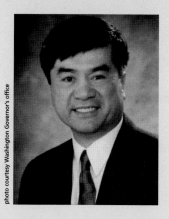

photo courtesy Washington Governor's office

An Immigrant's Story

Gary Locke's family immigrated to Washington from China. He grew up in Seattle, where he worked in his parents' grocery store. He studied hard in school, and graduated with honors from Franklin High School. With a combination of scholarships, part-time jobs, and government financial aid, he was able to go to Yale University. Then he went to law school in Boston. After he graduated, he came back to Seattle and began his career as a lawyer. In 1982, he was elected to the state House of Representatives, where he became chair of the House committee in charge of writing the state budget.

In 1996, he was elected Governor of Washington –the first person of color to be our governor, and the first Chinese-American in the history of the U. S. to be a governor.

While he was Governor, he made a trip to China to promote trade with our state. He was surprised to find out that he was a huge celebrity in China. When he went to the village his family came from, thousands of people lined the road to greet him, and children tossed flowers to honor his arrival.

vote and actually conduct elections.) The Secretary of State is also responsible for publishing the state voters' pamphlet, which is mailed to all the voters in the state before each election. The voters' pamphlet contains statements from candidates for state offices, and information about other issues that people vote on. The Secretary of State is also in charge of registering corporations and charities in the state, and keeping the state archives. The archives house all the historic documents of state government. (The archives web site is at www.secstate.wa.gov/archives.)

Like the Lieutenant Governor, the Secretary of State can also pursue his or her own agenda. In recent years, the Secretary of State has acted as a kind of ambassador for the state in other countries, and worked to improve relations between the state and Indian tribes.

The State Treasurer manages the state's cash and debts. She or he has to make sure that the state maintains a good credit rating, so that when the state wants to borrow money, it gets low interest rates.

Our Attorney General takes up a smoking controversy

Washington is a national leader in adopting laws to protect children and adults from the deadly effects of tobacco smoke. The legislature has passed laws that forbid selling tobacco to minors, tax cigarettes to make them very expensive, and create smoke-free areas so people are not exposed to secondhand smoke.

There is a growing movement all over the country to ban smoking in public places.

Some local governments, such as Pierce County, have banned smoking in bars and restaurants. This has caused a huge controversy, because some cities within the county don't want to do this.

In 1996, Christine Gregoire, Washington's Attorney General, filed a lawsuit against the tobacco companies because they were illegally trying to get minors to buy and use cigarettes. They were also violating Washington's consumer protection and antitrust laws. Forty-five other states also sued the industry. Our Attorney General was the lead negotiator of the final settlement in 1998. The states won the lawsuit, and now tobacco companies have to give $4.5 billion to our state over the next twenty-five years. The tobacco companies have to give money to the other states, too.

In our state, the governor and the legislature decide how the money will be spent. The state Department of Health uses some of the money to prevent kids from becoming addicted to tobacco, and to help adults quit smoking. Some of the money goes into the state's Basic Health Plan to help low-income people get health care.

Tobacco use is the leading cause of preventable death in the United States. The American Lung Association estimates that 440,000 Americans die every year from tobacco-related illnesses.

For more information about the Tobacco Prevention and Control Program, visit the web site at:

www.doh.wa,gov/ tobacco/default.htm

TV images from an anti-smoking campaign funded from the lawsuit.

Most kids who smoke think they'll quit within 5 years. But 70% are still smoking.

photos courtesy of the Washington State Department of Health

The State Auditor makes sure that everyone in state and local government follows the rules for how the public's tax dollars are spent.

The Attorney General is in charge of the state's own staff of lawyers. These lawyers represent state agencies when they have legal disputes. If a state law is challenged in court, they defend the law. They also protect consumers from fraud, and represent the state in major lawsuits. For example, our attorney general was a leader in suing the tobacco companies, and winning billions of dollars for our state to help pay for the health care costs of smokers, and to run campaigns to persuade people not to smoke.

The Superintendent of Public Education is in charge of the state's responsibilities for public schools. She does not have direct authority over schools – locally elected school boards do. But she is responsible for distributing state funds to schools, and for implementing state laws that establish academic standards that spell out what students should know and be able to do at each grade level. Her office provides expert advice to local school leaders and teachers about how to keep improving public schools.

The Commissioner of Public Lands is in charge of millions of acres of state-owned land. Most of this land was deeded to the state by the federal government when Washington gained statehood. The land includes large forests that are logged to earn money for special purposes such as building public schools, maintaining the state capitol, and building state hospitals. The Commissioner runs a big state agency called the Department of Natural Resources, and chairs the Forest Practices Board, which makes rules about how private landowners log their lands. The Department of Natural Resources also fights forest fires.

The Insurance Commissioner is in charge of making sure that insurance companies treat customers fairly, and that insurance companies follow the rules. The Commissioner also proposes legislation to correct problems with insurance companies.

The Judiciary

When someone is accused of breaking the law, Washington courts decide whether the person is innocent or guilty. If the person is found guilty, the court also decides what the punishment should be. To make this decision the judge (and sometimes a jury)

Charles Z. Smith is regarded as Washington's first African-American state Supreme Court Justice. His mother was African American and his father was an immigrant from Cuba, and Smith always remembered both his immigrant and African American roots.

Smith was born in Florida. He came to Seattle to attend the University of Washington School of Law. He was one of only four students of color in his class – and the only one who graduated in 1955.

He worked as a prosecutor, a judge, as a news commentator on radio and TV, and as a professor. Then in 1988, Governor Booth Gardner appointed him to fill a vacancy on the state Supreme Court. He served three terms.

He was an advocate for fairness for people of color, and also a leader in the American Baptist Churches, USA. He was appointed by President Clinton to serve on the U. S. Commission on International Freedom of Religion.

listens to people on both sides of the case (witnesses), who swear to tell the truth. Lying in a court is a crime called perjury, and people who commit perjury can be sent to jail for it. After they have listened to all the witnesses, the judge or the jury makes a decision.

There are two kinds of court cases: civil and criminal. A civil case is a dispute between two people – for instance, between a landlord and a renter, or between a husband and wife who want a divorce, or between a group of environmentalists and a company that wants to harvest trees in a forest.

In a criminal case, the two sides are the person accused of the crime and the government.

Criminal offenses are things like driving while drunk, robbery, or hitting someone. Criminal cases include both very small and very large crimes – everything from driving too fast to killing someone.

There are several levels of courts. The lowest level is the municipal and district courts. (A court is called a *municipal court* if it's run by a town or city, and a *district court* if it's run by a county – but both do the same things.) These courts handle things like traffic tickets, and small crimes, called *misdemeanors*, for which the penalty is less than one year in jail. When people are convicted of misdemeanors, they often just pay a fine, especially if it's for a driving violation like speeding or parking in the wrong place. If they are sentenced to jail, they are locked up in local jails, not state prisons. Municipal and district courts also handle smaller civil matters. They operate "small claims court" where people can sue for collection of debts up to $2,500.

There are two kinds of court cases: civil and criminal. A civil case is a dispute between two people. In a criminal case, the two sides are the person accused of the crime and the government.

The middle level of courts are called superior courts. These are the courts that handle most civil cases, including divorce, child custody, and other family matters. Superior court includes juvenile court, where kids are prosecuted if they are accused of a crime.

Superior courts also handle more serious crimes, called *felonies*. People who are convicted of felonies are usually sent to state prisons. People who were convicted of crimes in a municipal or district court can also appeal to a superior court if they think the local court wasn't fair to them, or didn't follow the law correctly. Every county has a superior court, but some rural counties share judges because they don't need a full-time judge.

There are also three state appeals courts, located in Tacoma, Seattle, and Spokane. People go to these courts when they feel that a superior court decision was unfair or not legally correct. When people appeal to these courts, the court doesn't listen to all the witnesses all over again; they just read the record of the earlier trial and listen to the lawyers for the parties involved explain why they thought the decision was or was not consistent with the law. Then the appellate court decides whether the lower court ruling was correct or not.

The top court for the state is the State Supreme Court, which consists of nine justices and is located in Olympia. The Supreme Court hears appeals from the lower courts. Unlike the other courts, the Supreme Court can decide which cases they want to hear. If they think a the lower court's decision was correct, they can decide not to take

University of Washington Libraries, Special Collections, neg UW 23531

Takuji Yamashita graduated from the University of Washington School of Law in 1902, but he was not permitted to practice as a lawyer because he wasn't a U. S. citizen. At that time, people from Asian countries were not allowed to become U. S. citizens. That law wasn't changed until 1952, and Mr. Yamashita died just a few years later. In 2001, several legal groups petitioned the Washington State Supreme Court to acknowledge the injustice of this by inducting Mr. Yamashita as a lawyer. The Court agreed to do this. A special ceremony was held, and members of Mr. Yamashita's family came all the way from Japan to attend.

up the case. (There is one exception to this: the Supreme Court is required to review all cases where a person has been sentenced to death.)

The Supreme Court's most important job is deciding exactly what state laws mean, and whether they are consistent with what our state constitution says. If a law violates the constitution, the Supreme Court can declare it *unconstitutional*, and the law is thrown out.

When people go to court, there is a very formal process (called a *trial*) for hearing both sides of a case. If a person is accused of a crime, that person has the right to a lawyer. If he or she can't afford a lawyer, one is appointed for them, and the county government pays for it. The state or local government also has a lawyer to present the evidence against the person being accused of a crime. The government's lawyer is called a *prosecutor*.

People who are accused of a crime have a right to a trial by jury, which means they can ask that a group of ordinary citizens listen to their case and decide if they are guilty or innocent.

People in civil cases can also request a jury. In civil cases, the jury is made up of six people rather than twelve, and the person who requests it has to pay a fee.

Sometimes, though, people don't ask for a jury; they trust the judge to make a fair decision. When a jury is needed, the court calls on local citizens to serve a jurors. They select people at random for jury duty, usually from lists of registered voters and licensed drivers. When citizens are called to serve on a jury, they are required to do so unless they have a good reason why they can't – for instance, if they have to take care of a sick relative, or they will be away on a trip. Jury duty is considered one of the obligations of being a good citizen.

All the judges in Washington are elected. But when a superior court or appeals court judge quits or retires in the middle of a term, the governor appoints someone to replace her until the next election. Then the person the governor appoints usually runs for the office, and usually gets elected. In fact,

In criminal prosecutions the accused shall have the right to...appear and defend in person, and by counsel, to demand the nature and cause of the accusation against him ...to meet the witness against him face to face ...to compel the attendance of witnesses on his behalf, to have a speedy public trial by an impartial jury."

ARTICLE I, SECTION 22
WASHINGTON STATE
CONSTITUTION

photo by Steve Bloom, April 6, 2004, reprinted courtesy *The Olympian*

it's a tradition for judges to do this, because a lot of people believe that the public is more likely to get a well-qualified judge if the governor makes the choice. This is a difficult issue because on the one hand, people want the right to elect judges, but, on the other hand, most of us really don't know which lawyers will make good judges.

There are special rules for people who run for judge that make this even more complicated. Candidates for judge aren't supposed to know who contributes to their campaigns, because we want judges to be fair, and not to grant favors to their con-tributors. Candidates for judge are also not supposed to talk about controversial issues that they might be called on to deal with in court. So in a campaign for a judgeship, voters don't have much to go on except the person's reputation and their qualifications. And since most of us don't spend a lot of time with lawyers, we may not know anything about the person's reputation, or have a good sense of whether they are qualified. When this happens, people often vote for judges because their name sounds familiar, or they might just not vote at all for these positions.

To try to improve the public's knowledge of candidates for judge, the state's Office of the Administrator for the Courts publishes a voters' guide. It isn't mailed to all voters; it is tucked into local newspapers. It is also online at **www.courts.wa.gov.**

In 1889, the first Supreme Court of Washington had 5 justices.

Washington is the first state in the nation to have 5 women sitting as judges on its Supreme Court.

6 Tribal governments today

In 1989, Washington's governor and representatives of many Indian tribes signed the Centennial Accord. (The state centennial was the 100th anniversary of Washington becoming a state.) The Centennial Accord said that state government would respect the sovereignty of the tribes – that is, it would respect Indian tribes' right to govern themselves.

photo courtesy Debbie Preston, Northwest Indian Fisheries Commission

This simple statement meant a lot to tribes. It meant that the state and the tribes would have a "government-to-government" relationship – a relationship between equals. Instead of trying to impose its rules on Indians, the state promised to work more closely with tribal governments, to respect the terms of the treaties and tribal laws, and to educate state employees about tribes and their governments. One example of this is the new way the state Department of Transportation works with tribes. The agency has hired a person to act as a liaison (go-between) with the tribes, so that when roads that cross reservations are to be built or improved, tribal governments are involved in all of the decisions about what will be done.

Federally recognized tribes

Chehalis Confederated Tribes

Confederated Tribes of the Colville Reservation

Cowlitz Tribe

Hoh Tribe

Jamestown S'Klallam Tribe

Kalispel Tribe

Lower Elwha Klallam Tribe

Lummi Nation

Makah Tribe

Muckleshoot Tribe

Nisqually Tribe

Nooksack Tribe

Port Gamble S'Klallam Tribe

Puyallup Tribe

Quileute Tribe

Quinault Nation

Samish Nation

Sauk-Suiattle Tribe

Shoalwater Bay Tribe

Skokomish Tribe

Snoqualmie Tribe

Spokane Tribe

Squaxin Island Tribe

Stillaguamish Tribe

Suquamish Tribe

Swinomish Tribe

The Tulalip Tribes

Upper Skagit Tribe

Yakama Nation

Non-Federally recognized Indian tribes

Note: Washington State does not have state-recognized tribes, as some states do. The following tribes are landless, non-federally recognized. Some are categorized as non-profit corporations; some are waiting for federal recognition. All have requested inclusion on this list.

Chinook Tribe**

Duwamish Tribe**

Kikiallus Indian nation

Marietta Band of Nooksak Tribe

Snohomish Tribe

Snoqualmoo Tribe

Steilacoom Tribe

**Pending Federal Recognition

Non-Washington Federally recognized Indian tribes with ceded territories in Washington state

Coeur d'Alene Tribe

Nez Perce Tribe

Confederated Tribes of the Umatilla Indian Reservation

Confederated Tribes of Warm Springs

Still, the tribes and the state government have a lot of work to do to make this new relationship smoother. Most people who work in state government still don't know very much about the history or culture of Indian tribes, or about what's in the treaties. So the Governor's Office of Indian Affairs provides special training for state employees on these topics, and on what it means to have a government-to-government relationship.

Today, tribes are also working hard to improve their governments so that they can provide essential services to their members. Health clinics, services for the elderly and people with disabilities, child welfare services, law enforcement, and schools and colleges are being created. Tribal governments are working with other governments to protect and restore salmon runs and improve the health of rivers and streams. Tribes are also opening new museums and working to preserve their history and renew their cultural traditions.

Squaxin Island Museum, Library and Resource Center

The Boldt decision

When Washington Indian nations signed treaties with the federal government, they gave up a lot of land, but they kept the right to hunt, fish and gather in all their "usual and accustomed places" – many of which were not on the reservations. At the time the treaties were signed, no one thought this would be a problem. But the population of settlers grew larger than anyone dreamed, and so did the number of white people who fished for a living. In fact, fishing became a major industry. Soon Indians were prevented from fishing in the places where they had fished for thousands of years. State agents arrested Indians caught fishing off their reservations, and took away their boats and fishing nets.

In the 1960s, Indian fishers began to protest this violation of their treaty rights. Many people (including some famous movie stars) came to support them, and news of these protests brought the issue to the attention of the public. Finally,

---

In 1968, African-American civil rights activist and comedian Dick Gregory, a supporter of Indian treaty rights, served time in the Thurston County jail for illegal net fishing on the Nisqually River.

---

the U. S. government acted to protect Indian rights by suing the state of Washington to allow Indians to fish.

In 1974, George Boldt, a federal judge, ruled that the Indians were right: the treaties said they had the right to fish "in common with" everyone else. Judge Boldt looked at an 1828 dictionary to see what the phrase "in common with" would have meant to the people who signed the treaties, and concluded that it meant Indians should have half of the salmon. He also ruled that Indian tribes should be partners with the state in managing and protecting salmon. The Boldt decision was a big victory for Indians – and in the long run, a big victory for salmon, too.

Today, tribal governments have a lot of people working to restore streams and rivers that have been polluted or damaged during the last century. Tribes have also helped educate the public about the connection between healthy rivers, healthy salmon, and healthy people.

The Boldt decision is famous because it confirmed that the treaties have to be respected. It encouraged tribes all over the U. S. (and native people in other countries) to insist on their rights. It also led to a flowering of Indian culture in our state, because the salmon are a central part of Indian life. Many Indians who had moved away from their reservations came home again. The Boldt decision, more than any other event, made it clear to everyone that Indian culture, history, and identity are here to stay.

Salmon ceremony, Tulalip tribe

Tribal governments are not like state government, or like local governments. They are unique, because they are governments for nations within a nation. Originally, the idea of the treaties was that the federal government should protect these "domestic dependent nations" from state governments. (In the case of fishing rights, that's what happened: the federal government sued the state to win recognition of the tribes' right to harvest fish, which was spelled out in treaties.)

Today, however, tribal governments are more like state government than they are like local governments, and it helps to understand what tribal governments can do if you compare them to states. For instance, tribes can run casinos because casinos are

A leader who brings people together

Billy Frank grew up on the Nisqually Reservation near Olympia. His dad, who lived to be 104, told him many stories that he had heard from his parents about what happened during "treaty times," when the reservation was created.

Billy was 14 when he was arrested for the first time by state game wardens for fishing. He became one of the leaders of the Indian fishing rights movement in the 1960s and early 1970s. He led "fish-ins" in the Nisqually River that attracted a lot of attention, and the support of many non-Indians. He was arrested many times.

Eventually, the fish-ins resulted in the court case that led to the Boldt decision – the court decision that said Indians have a right to half of the salmon that are caught each year, and that tribes and the state should share responsibility for taking care of salmon.

In 1975, Billy Frank helped create the Northwest Indian Fisheries Commission. The Commission helps tribes develop fisheries management plans, and "speaks for the salmon" in dealings with state government. Since the Boldt decision, tribes have developed hatcheries, restored streams and rivers that had been polluted or damaged, and worked together with state government to plan for restoring runs of salmon that have been depleted.

It has been hard for the tribes and the state to change from being enemies to being partners in caring for salmon. Billy Frank's leadership is a big part of what made that change possible, and what keeps it moving forward. He has received many awards and honors for doing this.

Today, Billy Frank is still telling his son the stories his dad told to him.

photo courtesy Northwest Indian Fisheries Commission

A leader who wove together the past and the future

Hazel Pete (1914-2003) was a member of the Chehalis Indian Tribe, which is located near Centralia. Although Hazel grew up during a time when American Indian people were not allowed to practice their native cultures, she devoted almost her entire adult life to learning, teaching, living, and celebrating the ways of her ancestors. She also came from a family that was very poor, but she never let that stop her from achieving the goals that she set for herself.

When Hazel was young, much of her life was spent living apart from her parents. She was sent to boarding schools run by the federal government where students were not allowed to speak their native languages or practice their own spiritual traditions. In the 1920s, very few Native American children attended schools with white children.

After graduating from high school in 1932, Hazel enrolled in another boarding school in Santa Fe, New Mexico. This school represented a change in federal policy; it actually encouraged people to preserve at least some of their native cultures. Hazel was one of the first students to enroll in a special program for the study of Indian arts and crafts. As a child, she had watched her grandmothers carefully craft beautifully woven baskets of all shapes and sizes from materials they gathered on the reservation. Hazel become a master basket maker, and taught people from many tribes how to make them, too. Eventually, people from all over the United States and the world traveled to the Chehalis reservation to buy Hazel Pete's baskets. Hazel Pete's greatest legacy was the role she played as a teacher. She taught arts and crafts in several boarding schools. She then returned to the Chehalis reservation, where she learned all she could about her tribe. For many years, she gave presentations in the local public schools. Wearing traditional clothing, she read Chehalis legends to students, sang songs to them, and tried to help them learn about Indian history and culture.

legal in the United States. Casinos are legal in the state of Nevada, because the Nevada state government chose to make them legal. Similarly, many tribal governments have chosen to make casinos legal on their lands. The federal and state governments regulate tribal casinos, but it is the tribes' right to operate them.

Many tribes are using money earned by tribal casinos to pay for government services to their members. Tribal casinos are a very important source of new jobs and income for tribes, and for nearby communities. Tribes also donate money from casinos to charities and community projects that help everyone.

Money from casinos is important because tribal governments have not had much of a tax base. Although some tribes have taxed tribal fishing and logging, most tribes didn't really have much to tax. They had to rely on very limited amounts of money from the federal government. In the treaties, Indians were promised health and education

An amazing beginning, a remarkable life

photo courtesy Virginia Beavert

Virginia Beavert was born in 1921 in a bear cave in the Blue Mountains. Her parents had gone hunting, and got caught in an early snow storm. She grew up on a cattle and horse ranch near Zillah. As a child, she learned the Yakama language from her family, and the traditional ways of using and preserving fish, native plants, roots, and berries. She graduated from Toppenish High School, and has fond memories of a circle of friends that included Native American, Caucasian, Japanese-American and Mexican-American girls. She served in the military during World War II, and then worked at Hanford, cared for her family, and worked in a hospital.

In 1974, at the age of 53, she graduated from Central Washington University. She became a member of the Yakama Tribal Council. She was often critical of the Council's actions, and so she helped push for a Code of Ethics that spelled out proper behavior for Council members. She often traveled to Washington, D. C. to represent the tribe. Now she teaches at Heritage College in Toppenish, and is working on creating a dictionary of the Yakama language, which is called Sahaptin. (Sahaptin was actually spoken by several tribes, and each tribe had its own version of it, called a dialect.) She is dedicated to preserving this language because it is such an important part of the Yakama culture and heritage. She is a beloved Elder of the Tribe, and an honorary member of the League of Women Voters.

Herman Williams (left) and Dale Reiner. Herman, Chair of the Tulalip Tribe, gave a blanket to Dale to honor him and his farming family for their salmon restoration work on Haskell Slough, which runs through Dale's property. Dale is a 5th generation farmer in the Skykomish Valley. He raises cattle and Christmas trees.

services "in perpetuity" (which means forever), but they often didn't get them. Many tribal councils met in church basements or school classrooms until the1970s or 1980s because they didn't have enough money to build a place to house their government

Most tribes that have casinos also use some of the money they earn to start other tribal enterprises. They want to have different kinds of businesses to provide a wider variety of jobs for tribal members, and a broader base of financial support for tribal government.

Tribal governments are not all alike. Most tribes have a tribal constitution that defines the structure of the government, but some do not. Each tribe also sets the rules about who is considered a tribal member. Most tribes have an elected tribal council as their central leadership. Usually, the chair of the tribal council is the person who speaks for the tribe.

Tribal councils are advised by a lot of committees made up of tribal members. The committees study issues and give the tribal council advice. In some tribes, the committees have the power to make decisions on their own. Committees deal with tribal membership, housing, fisheries, elections, programs for children and elders, hunting, education, and culture.

Tribal councils and committees do just what Indians did before settlers came: they spend a lot of time talking – and listening – to try to find solutions to problems that everyone can agree on. Even though the structure of many tribal governments is non-traditional, the cultural habit of seeking consensus is still very strong. This sometimes frustrates people from other governments, because they are used to meeting deadlines, no matter what. In many tribal governments, it is more important to take time to reach agreement than it is to meet a deadline. Tribes want to make sure that everyone is heard, and that everyone's needs are met.

Measuring water height for a flood study along the Nooksak River.

Today, tribal governments have more and more paid staff, because they are taking on more responsibility and creating more programs to help tribal members and their communities. In fact, tribes actually employ more fisheries

biologists than the state does. Tribal government staff carry out the policies set by the tribal government committees and the tribal council.

Suquamish tribal members paddle their canoe through the breakers.

Most tribes have their own police and courts. Tribal police and courts can deal with crimes committed by tribal members (or members of other tribes), but when non-Indian people commit crimes on reservations, other police agencies are usually called in. This has been the source of a lot of confusion and conflict. In some places, tribal police and county sheriffs are working together to overcome these problems, and to share responsibility for keeping the whole community safe. They have "cross deputized" each other, so that tribal and non-tribal police can act on each others' behalf.

As tribal governments grow, many tribes need more employees, managers, and leaders, so tribal governments are investing more in scholarships to encourage young tribal members to go to college, and to learn the skills they will need to lead tribal governments and run tribal enterprises in the years to come.

Despite the many positive changes occurring in Indian country, Indian tribes and reservations still have many people in poverty, especially in rural areas. A full recovery from centuries of defeat, discrimination, and broken promises will take more time, and more work by both tribal and non-tribal governments and all people of goodwill. It will also take more education of non-Indians about the history, culture and status of the tribes.

photo courtesy Debbie Preston, Northwest Indian Fisheries Commission

Quileute students looking for birds, La Push

7 Local government: counties, cities, towns and special districts

There are 281 cities and towns, 39 counties and 1700 special purpose districts in Washington.

Local governments provide services right up to the driveway and even inside most peoples' houses: the streets that people live on, the water that comes out of the faucets, the sewers that take away everything that goes down the drains, and the garbage service that picks up trash (and probably recyclables) are all provided by local governments. (Of course, some people who live in the country have their own well for water and their own septic system for wastewater – but even they probably rely on local government for the road to their house, and for the snowplow that keeps their road clear in the winter.)

Local governments also keep us safe in many ways. Building inspectors make sure that the houses we live in and the schools we attend are built properly, and won't fall down in an earthquake. Health departments make sure that restaurants are clean, and that they don't serve food that will make us sick. Local police and sheriffs protect us from crime; fire departments put out fires and promote fire prevention. If someone is so mentally ill that they are a danger to themselves or others, we can call a local government employee called a County-Designated Mental Health Professional for help. These are just a few examples of important local government services.

Local governments are smallest, closest to us, and usually the first place we turn when we need help. Because they are so close to us, local governments are also the easiest for citizens to participate in. If we want to change a state or national law, we might have to send letters or travel to the state or national capitol. But if we want to change something at the local level, we might be able to talk to a local elected official when we run into them at the grocery store or at a Little League game.

Local governments shape the communities we live in. If a community has nice parks, safe streets, and clean water, it's because its county and city governments and special districts are doing a good job. And when local government is doing a good job, people take pride in their community and work together to make it even better.

Counties

Washington has 39 counties.

Counties were created during the years when Washington was a territory (1853 – 1889), because people needed local services that the territorial government was just too far away to provide. At that time, there weren't very many cities or towns, so the county

Okanogan County
Named for an Indian tribe, the county was organized by the territorial legislature on February 1, 1888. The name is derived from the Indian word "okanagen," meaning "rendezvous," (a meeting place) and was applied originally to the river's head at Osoyoos Lake where Indians gathered annually to catch and cure fish, to trade, and to hold potlatches. The name was gradually applied to the river and to the tribe that lived along its banks.

map courtesy of Washington State Department of Ecology

Population by County (2001)

County/population	City/Town	Population
Adams 16,600	Hatton	119
	Lind	580
	Othello	5,895
	Ritzville	1,745
	Washtucna	260
Asotin 20,700	Asotin	1,095
	Clarkston	7,380
Benton 144,800	Benton City	2,720
	Kennewick	55,780
	Prosser	4,865
	Richland	39,350
	West Richland	8,735
Chelan 67,100	Cashmere	3,070
	Chelan	3,535
	Entiat	975
	Leavenworth	2,080
	Wenatchee	27,930
Clallam 64,800	Forks	3,145
	Port Angeles	18,420
	Sequim	4,370
Clark 352,600	Battle Ground	10,040
	Camas	12,970
	La Center	1,735
	Ridgefield	2,175
	Vancouver	145,300
	Washougal	8,790
	Yacolt	1,065
Columbia 4,100	Dayton	2,715
	Starbuck	130
Cowlitz 93,900	Castle Rock	2,125
	Kalama	1,840
	Kelso	11,860
	Longview	35,100
Cowlitz/Clark	Woodland	3,875
Douglas 32,800	Bridgeport	2,080
	East Wenatchee	5,770
	Mansfield	321
	Rock Island	865
	Waterville	1,170
Douglas/Grant/Okanogan	Coulee Dam	1,045
Ferry 7,300	Republic	990

County/population	City/Town	Population
Franklin 50,400	Connell	2,970
	Kahlotus	215
	Mesa	440
	Pasco	33,010
Garfield 2,400	Pomeroy	1,520
Grant 75,900	Coulee City	600
	Electric City	950
	Ephrata	6,895
	George	535
	Grand Coulee	926
	Hartline	135
	Krupp	65
	Mattawa	2,820
	Moses Lake	15,210
	Quincy	5,165
	Royal City	1,825
	Soap Lake	1,730
	Warden	2,565
	Wilson Creek	244
Grays Harbor 68,500	Aberdeen	16,490
	Cosmopolis	1,595
	Elma	3,050
	Hoquiam	9,035
	McCleary	1,445
	Montesano	3,325
	Oakville	680
	Ocean Shores	3,930
	Westport	2,150
Island 72,400	Coupeville	1,735
	Langley	970
	Oak Harbor	20,060
Jefferson 26,100	Port Townsend	8,430
King 1,758,300	Algona	2,500
	Auburn	43,985
	Beaux Arts Village	310
	Bellevue	111,500
	Black Diamond	4,015
	Burien	31,830
	Carnation	1,920
	Clyde Hill	2,900
	Covington	13,840
	Des Moines	29,600

County/population	City/Town	Population
King (con't)	Duvall	4,860
	Enumclaw	11,180
	Federal Way	83,890
	Hunts Point	455
	Issaquah	12,950
	Kent	81,900
	Kirkland	45,770
	Lake Forest Park	13,160
	Maple Valley	14,590
	Medina	2,990
	Mercer Island	21,970
	Newcastle	7,815
	Normandy Park	6,405
	North Bend	4,755
	Redmond	45,490
	Renton	51,140
	SeaTac	25,380
	Seattle	568,100
	Shoreline	53,150
	Skykomish	215
	Snoqualmie	3,416
	Tukwila	17,230
	Woodinville	9,210
	Yarrow Point	1,010
King/Pierce	Milton	5,820
	Pacific	5,525
King/Snohomish	Bothell	30,470
Kitsap 233,400	Bainbridge Island	20,740
	Bremerton	37,260
	Port Orchard	7,810
	Poulsbo	6,965
Kittitas 34,000	Cle Elum	1,755
	Ellensburg	15,460
	Kittitas	1,105
	Roslyn	1,017
	South Cle Elum	543
Klickitat 19,300	Bingen	675
	Goldendale	3,745
	White Salmon	2,215
Lewis 69,500	Centralia	14,950
	Chehalis	7,015
	Morton	1,040
	Mossyrock	490
	Napavine	1,352
	Pe Ell	660
	Toledo	684
	Vader	605
	Winlock	1,337

County/population	City/Town	Population
Lincoln 10,200	Almira	300
	Creston	251
	Davenport	1,735
	Harrington	425
	Odessa	960
	Reardan	610
	Sprague	505
	Wilbur	920
Mason 49,600	Shelton	8,470
Okanogan 39,700	Brewster	2,205
	Conconully	190
	Elmer City	270
	Nespelem	210
	Okanogan	2,480
	Omak	4,730
	Oroville	1,670
	Pateros	640
	Riverside	330
	Tonasket	1,010
	Twisp	955
	Winthrop	350
Pacific 21,000	Ilwaco	950
	Long Beach	1,385
	Raymond	2,975
	South Bend	1,805
Pend Oreille 11,800	Cusick	210
	Ione	475
	Metaline	160
	Metaline Falls	225
	Newport	2,020
Pierce 713,400	Bonney Lake	9,980
	Buckley	4,330
	Carbonado	650
	DuPont	2,855
	Eatonville	2,040
	Edgewood	9,220
	Fife	4,820
	Fircrest	5,890
	Gig Harbor	6,485
	Lakewood	58,190
	Orting	4,015
	Puyallup	33,900
	Roy	367
	Ruston	740
	South Prairie	430
	Steilacoom	6,085
	Sumner	8,585
	Tacoma	194,500
	University Place	30,190
	Wilkeson	417

County/population	City/Town	Population
San Juan 14,400	Friday Harbor	2,020
Skagit 104,100	Anacortes	14,840
	Burlington	6,995
	Concrete	790
	Hamilton	325
	La Conner	765
	Lyman	410
	Mount Vernon	26,460
	Sedro-Woolley	8,700
Skamania 9,900	North Bonneville	586
	Stevenson	1,205
Snohomish 618,600	Arlington	12,770
	Brier	6,440
	Darrington	1,307
	Edmonds	39,590
	Everett	95,990
	Gold Bar	2,035
	Granite Falls	2,540
	Index	160
	Lake Stevens	6,590
	Lynnwood	34,010
	Marysville	26,770
	Mill Creek	11,970
	Monroe	14,210
	Mountlake Terrace	20,370
	Mukilteo	18,340
	Snohomish	8,565
	Stanwood	3,975
	Sultan	3,775
	Woodway	945
Spokane 422,400	Airway Heights	4,490
	Cheney	9,200
	Deer Park	3,035
	Fairfield	591
	Latah	205
	Medical Lake	3,820
	Millwood	1,650
	Rockford	509
	Spangle	295
	Spokane	195,700
	Waverly	138
Stevens 40,300	Chewelah	2,200
	Colville	5,010
	Kettle Falls	1,550
	Marcus	156
	Northport	312
	Springdale	285

County/population	City/Town	Population
Thurston 210,200	Bucoda	635
	Lacey	31,600
	Olympia	42,530
	Rainier	1,485
	Tenino	1,460
	Tumwater	12,770
	Yelm	3,420
Wahkiakum 3,800	Cathlamet	560
Walla Walla 55,200	College Place	7,945
	Prescott	315
	Waitsburg	1,205
	Walla Walla	29,500
Whatcom 170,600	Bellingham	68,890
	Blaine	3,855
	Everson	2,050
	Ferndale	8,925
	Lynden	9,285
	Nooksack	918
	Sumas	995
Whitman 40,300	Albion	625
	Colfax	2,835
	Colton	390
	Endicott	342
	Farmington	150
	Garfield	640
	LaCrosse	380
	Lamont	105
	Malden	215
	Oakesdale	420
	Palouse	1,015
	Pullman	24,540
	Rosalia	660
	St. John	513
	Tekoa	825
	Uniontown	340
Yakima 224,500	Grandview	8,410
	Granger	2,575
	Harrah	614
	Mabton	1,905
	Moxee	835
	Naches	703
	Selah	6,405
	Sunnyside	14,010
	Tieton	1,175
	Toppenish	8,975
	Union Gap	5,655
	Wapato	4,555
	Yakima	73,040
	Zillah	2,472

was the only local government for most people. Counties ran the schools, built the roads, hired the sheriffs and judges, and in some cases built hospitals. (In fact, in the early days, counties required all the men to work three days each year helping to build the roads.)

After Washington became a state, state government gradually took over some of the things counties had done. And as more cities and towns came into being, they also took over some of what the counties used to do. So the role of county governments has changed a lot – and is still changing as our population grows and more cities and towns are created.

What are social services?

Social services – also sometimes called human services – are a big part of what government does. These services include

- *Health care for people who have very low incomes*

- *Care for people who can't work, such as people with disabilities and the elderly*

- *Help for people who are poor and need help finding a job, or job training*

- *Housing for people who are poor and/or homeless*

- *Mental health care – both in the community, and in mental hospitals*

- *Treatment to overcome addiction to drugs, alcohol, or gambling*

- *Services to take care of babies, children and teens who are abused or neglected by their parents, or whose parents are too ill to take care of them*

- *Help for young people who've been in trouble with the law and who need to turn their lives in a better direction*

Providing these services gets very complicated, because governments at many levels are involved. For instance, the federal government and the state share responsibility for Medicaid, a huge program that provides health insurance to people who have low incomes. Many of those who

photo courtesy Family Policy Council

receive Medicaid are people who work full time, but don't make very much money. Others are people who can't work because of a disability, or because they are too old to work.

Many other social services are provided by complex partnerships between the state, county governments, and private and non-profit community organizations.

Nearly all social services are provided only to those who can't afford to buy them on their own. Governments have to decide how poor people should be before they get government help. At the same time, they have to figure out how much government can afford to spend on these services. People don't always get what they need, because sometimes the government doesn't have enough money.

Bats in Your House

When a bat in flies into someone's house, it's pretty scary, because bats sometimes carry rabies – a very bad disease that must be diagnosed and treated quickly to prevent someone from getting sick.

If this happens to you, you can call the county health department for advice. A person from the environmental health section will help

decide what to do. First, they will ask if anyone was bitten or scratched by the bat. Sometimes a bat bite is very small and cannot be seen, so they also ask if anyone was awakened or disturbed by the bat. If the answer is no, there is nothing to worry about.

If the answer is yes, and the bat is still available, the health department will test it to see if it is

has rabies. The bat most often is trapped by the home owner and then delivered to the local Animal Services facility to be prepared for rabies testing. The bat body has to be put in a special

shipping box and sent to the virology laboratory at the Washington State Health Department in Seattle. They do special tests on the bat's brain to see if it had rabies. If it did, the person who got bitten or scratched has to have shots to prevent the illness.

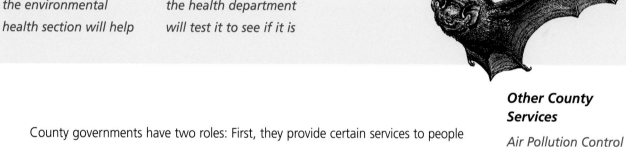

County governments have two roles: First, they provide certain services to people who live inside the county, but outside of any town or city. For instance, county sheriffs patrol the roads and respond to crimes committed within the county, but outside of towns or cities. Second, counties provide some services to everyone in the county, regardless of whether they live in a town or city or in what is called an *"unincorporated area"* – an area that isn't in a city or town. (This is explained more in the section on cities and towns.)

The services county governments provide for everyone in the county include collecting property taxes, protecting public health, providing human services (such as help for the elderly and people who are mentally ill), and conducting elections. County governments are also responsible for the superior and district courts, and the county jail.

Counties are usually governed by three elected Commissioners. Together, these three elected commissioners are called the County Commission. The County Commission

Other County Services

Air Pollution Control

Animal Services

Area Agency on Aging

Cooperative Extension Services

Courts

Financial Services

Transit

Marriage License

Medic One

Parks and Recreation

Public Health and Social Services

Sheriff

Waste Management

Water

King County, the largest county in Washington, was orignally named after William R. King, the vice president under Franklin Pierce. It was renamed in 1986 after civil rights leader Dr. Martin Luther King, Jr.

combines both executive and legislative functions of government. It is responsible for setting the county's budget and laws, and seeing that they are carried out.

According to the original state constitution, counties are also supposed to have several other elected officials:

The County Assessor decides how much property (land, buildings and business equipment) is worth. The value of the property determines how much tax the person who owns it has to pay; the more valuable the property, the more tax people pay.

The County Treasurer sends people bills for their property tax, and makes sure they pay it. Then he or she distributes the money – some goes to the state government, some to schools, and some to local governments. The Treasurer may also serve as the banker for some or all of the local governments in the county.

photo courtesy Leslie Hoge Design

Justin Amorratanasuchad at the Ballard Bowl

Your tax dollars at work . . . and play

Teens often wish they had more places to go to be with their friends. They also have a hard time finding places where they can skateboard. So in the last ten years or so, a lot of towns and cities have built skateparks – and a lot of young people have been involved in lobbying and raising money to get them built. In many communities, kids have also helped design them. Skateparks have become popular places for kids to meet and practice their skateboarding

skills. Often, older kids help younger kids learn. Kids appreciate having a place to go where there's no admission fee, and anyone can come.

Although skateparks are very popular, finding the money to build a skatepark can be difficult when towns or cities have tight budgets.

Here's a web site that has a list of all the skateparks in Washington: www.mrsc.org/Subjects/Planning/sktbdprk.aspx

For more information on how much skateparks cost and how different parks have different rules, check out the <u>AWC's Skateboard Facilities Survey</u> *link on this web site.*

How cities spend their money (2002)

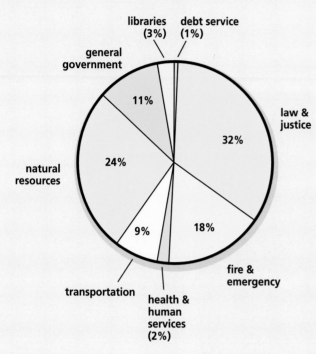

- law & justice **32%**
- general government **11%**
- libraries **(3%)**
- debt service **(1%)**
- natural resources **24%**
- transportation **9%**
- health & human services **(2%)**
- fire & emergency **18%**

Where city governments get their money (2002)

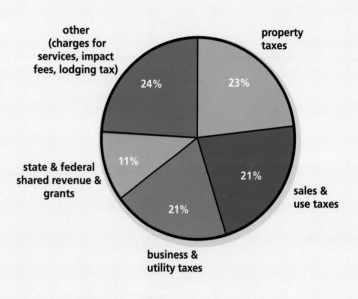

- property taxes **23%**
- other (charges for services, impact fees, lodging tax) **24%**
- state & federal shared revenue & grants **11%**
- sales & use taxes **21%**
- business & utility taxes **21%**

The County Auditor keeps records of who owns all the property in the county. He or she keeps records of all the registered voters, and runs the elections. And if you want to get married, it's the County Auditor who will issue your marriage license.

The County Sheriff is the chief law enforcement officer in the county. He or she is in charge of deputies who provide police services for those who live outside towns or cities. In some counties the Sheriff's deputies also provide police services inside cities. In most counties, the Sheriff is also in charge of the county jail.

The County Coroner investigates suspicious deaths to find out whether someone was murdered or died of natural causes.

The Governor Albert D. Rosellini Bridge, which connects Seattle and Bellevue across Lake Washingon, is the longest floating bridge in the world.

Art, government and controversy

Our national and state government – and many local governments – have commissions or agencies that support the arts. These agencies are usually a very small part of the budget, but people get very passionate about them. Supporters of the arts point out that art is vital to the health of our culture and our understanding of what it means to be human. They believe that government should actively support the arts with funding for local theater groups, dance troupes, painters, sculptors, museums and musicians. This is important to making art available to everyone, rather than just to those who can afford to buy art work. It helps communities produce and preserve art that is unique to their own culture, history and experience.

photo by YaM Studio, courtesy 4Culture
"Rain Forest Gates", 1999.
(c) Jean Whitesavage & Nick Lyle.
Hand-forged and painted steel entrance gates to King Street Center in Seattle, King County Public Art Collection

In some places, local governments require that one percent of the cost of any new government construction project be devoted to buying art that will be displayed in or around the new building or other facility. The new art that is purchased might be a piece of sculpture, or a mural, or a frieze that is part of the new building. But people argue passionately about art, and when government supports artists or buys art, there can be disagreements about what is "good" art. Some people get angry when their tax dollars are spent on art they don't personally like. The federal agency that supports the arts – the National Endowment for the Arts – has long been a major focus of such debates. Politics and art don't always mix well, but sometimes they are impossible to keep separate.

Here are web site addresses for a few state and local government arts commissions:

www.arts.wa.gov *The Washington State Arts Commission*

www.4Culture.org *4Culture (The Cultural Development Authority of King County)*

www.cityofseattle.net/arts/ *Seattle Mayor's Office of Arts and Cultural Affairs*

www.spokanearts.org/ *Spokane Arts Commission*

The County Clerk is in charge of keeping all the paperwork for the courts, and for helping people who want to get divorced, sue someone, or deal with other legal matters.

The County Prosecuting Attorney is in charge of representing the government in court when someone is accused of a crime. The Prosecutor also defends the county when it is sued, and provides legal advice to all the agencies of county government.

Superior court judges are also elected county officials. They preside over superior courts, which handle all serious crimes, and also all civil cases, such as divorces, child custody cases, and lawsuits. Superior courts include juvenile court, where kids are tried and sentenced if they commit a crime.

District court judges preside over the smaller courts that deal with minor crimes and traffic tickets. (Within cities and towns, there are similar small courts, called municipal courts.)

Did you know:

Seattle is home to the first revolving restaurant, which was built in 1961.

Everett is the site of the world's largest building, Boeing's final assembly plant.

When **Spokane** hosted the World's fair in 1974, it was the smallest city in size ever to do so.

A big city mayor has a very big job

photo courtesy the City of Spokane

As mayor of Spokane, Jim West directs the activities of more than 2,000 city employees and manages a $409 million annual budget.

Mayor West is a third-generation Spokanite. He has been an Army paratrooper, a police officer, a deputy sheriff, and a state legislator for 21 years (1982-2003). He has volunteered for many nonprofit and service organizations.

He ran for mayor while serving as Senate Majority leader and undergoing treatment for colon cancer.

Noting that 1973 was the last time Spokane re-elected a mayor, he says, "I don't have a lot of time to get a lot done." So he has moved quickly to implement his goals for an open, responsive and accountable government. In his first few months in office, he met every day with a group of city department heads, combined three city

departments into one to promote economic development, started new training programs for city employees to improve services to citizens. He wants to use his time in office to make sure Spokane has a sound government that can help the city grow and prosper.

He says becoming mayor of Spokane is a dream fulfilled.

photo courtesy Bill Wagner and *The Daily News* of Longview, WA

The Cookie Mayor

As a Mom, Barbara Larsen got involved in her children's schools, and that led her to serve for thirteen years on the local school board in Castle Rock, a town of about 2,200 people. She enjoyed public service, so when there was an open seat on the city council, she ran for it – and won. After ten years on the city council, she ran for mayor, and now she's in her second term.

While her children were growing up, she and her husband ran a dairy. For the past forty years, she has also been a foster mom who takes care of sick babies when their parents can't care for them. She takes care of them until their parents can take them back, or until the state's Child Protective Services office (a part of the Department of Social and Health Services) can find a permanent home for them. Over the years, she has cared for hundreds of babies.

She often takes babies – and cookies – to meetings of the city council.

However, not all counties are organized like this. The state constitution was amended in 1948 to allow counties (and cities) to do things their own way. To change the way local governments are organized, voters elect people called freeholders, and the freeholders write up a mini-constitution for the county or city. This mini-constitution is called a "home rule charter." Then everyone votes to accept or reject the charter. If the majority votes for it, then it is accepted.

Under a home rule charter, counties can change the number of elected officials and their duties. Most have chosen to separate the legislative and executive functions of government by having an elected County Executive and a County Council. They can also give local people the powers of the initiative and referendum. They cannot, however, change the job of the county prosecutor or the superior and district court judges, or the way the courts are organized.

Five counties have adopted home rule charters. They are Clallam, King, Pierce, Snohomish, and Whatcom. Taken together, these counties include about half of the state's population.

County Commissioners are elected in an interesting way. The county is divided into districts, and people in each district vote for their own commissioner in the primary election. Then, in the general (final) election, everyone in the county gets to vote on all the commissioners. In this way, every part of the county is assured of having someone to represent their area. But, because everyone in the county votes for all the Commissioners in the final election, the commissioners are reminded that they must serve not just their own district, but all the people in the county.

Cities and Towns

When someone asks you where you are from, you probably say the name of your town or city – or, if you live in the country, you probably say the name of the nearest town or city. You probably wouldn't say what county you are from.

People have special feelings about their towns and cities. We call the place where we grow up our "home town." We feel that we are a part of our home town, and it is a part of us. That's why people sometimes get so passionate about what town or city governments do; it's almost as important to us as what our families or the people in our neighborhoods do. We know that when our town or city government makes an important decision, it will have a direct effect on the place we call home.

Cities and towns are organized in a different way than counties. Counties are created by the state, and they can do only what the state says they can do. Cities and towns, however, are created by the people who live in them. When a group of people who live in a particular place decide that they want to be a city or a town, they can hold an election and vote to incorporate. This means that they create a municipal corporation. We usually think of a corporation as a big company like Boeing or Microsoft, but the word corporation can also refer to "a group of people combining into or acting as one body." (The word municipal just means a local unit of government, such as a town, village, or city.) So a municipal corporation is a legal term for a town or city. And an unincorporated area is a part of a county that isn't in a town.

The difference between a city and a town is size. A town has a population of less than 1,500 at the time it is incorporated. Among cities, there are two legal classifications: a first class city is one that has more than 10,000 people at the time it is incorporated, and a

> **The percentage of the state's population living in cities is now 61%— up from 52% in 1990.**

A mayor's life of public service

photo courtesy Trixanna Koch

As a child, Jesse Farias worked in the fields with his family. When he graduated from high school in 1963, he joined the army. Four years later in Vietnam, his group was ambushed while crossing a river. He was severely injured, and lost his legs. At the age of 22, Jesse began life in a wheel chair.

When he came back from Vietnam, he knew he would have to find work that used his brain – and for that, he would need a college degree. A friend helped him get a part-time job working for the state Employment Security Department to help support his

family while he went to school. Farias graduated from college in 1973, and began working full time for the state. In 1989, Governor Booth Gardner appointed him Director of Veteran's Affairs. Farias enjoyed the challenge of heading a state agency and was sorry to leave when Gardner's term ended. But he came back to Olympia again in 1997, when Governor Gary Locke appointed him to serve a term on the State Liquor Board.

Now retired, Farias serves his community as Mayor of Wapato.

second class city is one that had more than 1,500, but less than 10,000. In 2003, there were 281 towns or cities in Washington, but people are still creating new ones.

The state constitution sets out rules for how to create a city or town, and how its government should be organized. However, the constitution was amended (as it was for counties) to create home rule charters that allow cities more freedom about how they organize themselves.

There are three kinds of city or town governments. The differences have to do with how the legislative and executive functions are divided up. The two major ones are:

The mayor-council form of government consists of an elected mayor, who serves as the leader of the executive branch of city government, and an elected council, which serves as the legislative body.

In some cities, the mayor can veto laws passed by the council, but, like the state legislature, the council can override the veto. People call this the "strong mayor" form of government. When the mayor has no veto power, and when there are several other city-wide elected officials such as a city auditor or prosecutor, it's called a "weak mayor" form of government.

The council-manager form of government has an elected council, and the council members hire someone to be the city manager. The city manager works for the council. The city manager hires the rest of the city employees, and runs the day-to-day operations of the city or town. The council is not allowed to interfere in this work, but they can fire the city manager if they don't like the job he or she is doing. In this form of government, most of the work of the executive branch is done by the city manager, but the council (the legislative branch) has control over it.

The council-manager form of government was invented early in the 20th century by people who thought that local government should be run more like a business.

The third form of municipal government is only used by one town – Shelton. It has three elected commissioners who serve as city department directors. One is the Commissioner of Public Safety (who also serves as the mayor), one is the Commissioner of Finance and Accounting, and the third is Commissioner of Streets and Public Improvements.

The largest city in Washington is Seattle, with a population of 571,900 people...and the smallest is Krupp, with 65 people.

City and town governments vary a lot. As you can imagine, a city the size of Seattle, Spokane, or Tacoma needs a lot of services that a small town might not need or want. In cities and large towns, for instance, city government might run shelters and other programs to help homeless people, but in small or rural towns, these might not be needed.

The relationship between city and town governments and county governments also varies a lot. Sometimes smaller towns, and towns in rural counties, rely heavily on county government because the towns don't have much money. However, even in urban counties, sometimes the county government takes responsibility for big important things like public transit or sewage treatment that cross all the borders of towns and cities. This is true in King County, where only 15% of the population lives in unincorporated areas. If every city and town in King County had to run its own public bus system, you would have to get on and off the bus many times to cross the county, because you would have to change buses in every town you traveled through.

Cities, towns, and county governments work together on many issues. For instance, in a county that has several towns, the elected officials of the county government and the town governments might get together and decide to share an Animal Services Department to deal with stray dogs and cats. They might all contribute some money for this purpose and share responsibility for the county-wide agency. Or they might pool their money and then pay a private organization – like the Humane Society – to do the work. Having one animal control agency for the whole county will save everybody money.

County roads have to connect with city and town roads and streets, so everyone works together to plan for this, too. They also collaborate to figure out how towns and

Richland, Kennewick, and Pasco comprise the entity commonly called the Tri-Cities. The first two, located in Benton County, were initially small agricultural communities, while Pasco was the Franklin County seat and site of railroad yards. In 1943 the Atomic Energy Commission constructed a plutonium-producing facility, the Hanford Works, north of Richland. The three towns boomed and grew into one crescent-shaped population center extending along both banks of the Columbia River.

cities should grow, where new neighborhoods, shopping centers, and businesses should be built, and what land should be left open for forests, farming, parks, and other uses.

In big cities and in cities with a strong mayor form of government, being the mayor is a full-time job. The mayor's role is similar to the governor's: he or she is the boss of city departments, and can hire and fire department directors. The mayor also has a relationship with the city council that is similar to the governor's relationship with the state legislature. The Mayor can propose new laws or the city's annual budget, but the city council has to vote for it, and they can change it if they don't like the mayor's ideas. Together, the mayor and the city council have to work out their differences.

In small towns, and in towns with the council-manager form of government, being mayor means something quite different. In these governments, the mayor is one of the city council members. He or she leads council meetings, and represents the city at special events and ceremonies. Sometimes the mayor is a strong leader because she has a clear vision for what she want the town to be like, and is able to unite people to achieve that vision. In other cases, the mayor may be just a member of the council who holds the title of mayor.

Special purpose districts

When Washington was a territory, the territorial government divided counties into school districts. Today, Washington has 296 school districts. The voters in each school district elect five (in a few cases seven) school board members to govern their public schools. The biggest school district in the state is Seattle, which has nearly 50,000 students. The smallest is Benge, in Adams County, which has nine students in a two-room school.

School boards are responsible for the budgets and policies of local schools. There are a lot of state laws that set the basic rules for schools, but local school boards can add local graduation requirements, negotiate contracts with teachers, decide when and whether to build new schools, and what academic programs and sports will be offered.

Jurisdiction:

Power and control over a certain area. (For instance, if you ask a mayor of a city to solve a problem that is outside the city's borders, he or she might say, "That's not in my jurisdiction.")

About 80% of the money for schools comes from the state government, but the rest has to come from within the school district. To raise this money, school boards figure out how much money the schools need, and then ask people in the district to vote to tax themselves for that amount. This is called a school levy election. For a school levy to be approved, 60% of the voters have to vote for it. The taxes for school levies come from property tax on people's land, houses, and other buildings.

The school board also has to ask voters to tax themselves to help pay for building new schools or sports facilities. When they put a measure on the ballot to build something new, it's called a school bond election.

School districts are just one of many kinds of special purpose districts. Usually, a special purpose district has just one job – for example, running a port, providing sewage treatment, managing irrigation in a certain area, or building and maintaining a ball park.

There are over 1,400 special purpose districts in Washington, and they do an amazing variety of things. For instance, a Metropolitan Park District was set up in Tacoma in 1907 to create the Tacoma Zoo. There are cemetery districts, mosquito control districts, fire districts, library districts, and transit districts. Seattle even has a special purpose district to build and run a new monorail system.

In some cases, special purpose districts are created to provide a specific service (a fire department, for instance) in an unincorporated area of a county. In other cases, several counties might band together to create a multi-county transit district (such as Sound Transit, which serves King, Pierce, and Snohomish Counties).

Usually, special purpose districts are governed by elected boards, but sometimes they are governed by boards appointed by County Commissioners.

Probably the most famous special purpose district is the Washington State Major League Baseball Public Facilities District, which owns and manages Safeco Field in Seattle.

photo courtesy Ben VanHouten

Safeco Field, Seattle

8 What does it take to be a good citizen?

Usually when people talk about being a good citizen, the first thing that comes up is voting. That's because voting is the most basic act of citizenship. When immigrants become citizens, they nearly always take great pride in being able to vote. They are right to feel this way. There's really nothing more important than the act of marking a ballot and making an informed choice about how we want to shape our future, and who we want to lead us.

But voting is only part of the story. In fact, government is only a part of the story. To be good citizens, we have to think about the whole of our lives – about how we treat the people around us, how well we take care of the natural world, and what impact all our actions will have on the future.

To live in an open, democratic society, we have to accept that not everyone will share our beliefs. (When a society includes and embraces people who have a variety of backgrounds and beliefs, it's called *pluralism*.) In fact, it helps if we all enjoy this diversity. If we only spend time with people who think and act just like us, we would never hear about new ideas that might be better than our own. In the long history of human civilization, the most progress has always been made when people are exposed to new ideas, new ways of looking at things, and new insights – even if those new ways of thinking seem disturbing or difficult to understand at first.

But voting and being open to new ideas are just the beginning. Being a good citizen also requires striving to develop certain habits of mind and ways of living. Here's one list of traits and habits that contribute to good citizenship. You may think of others that should be added:

Try to be a person of good character.

Good people make good citizens. Being a good person means always trying to be kind and honest, to pay attention to other peoples' needs, to respect yourself and others, and to work hard. None of us is perfect, so we also need to cultivate the habit of facing up to our faults and striving to overcome them.

Love to learn.

The best way to help make the world a better place is to keep learning all you can about it. Knowledge is power. For instance, the more we know about salmon, rivers, and oceans, the more likely we will be able to save both the salmon and the natural world that sustains us.

Learn science.

In the 21st century, scientific discoveries will change our world in ways we can't yet understand. To make sure these changes benefit all of us, we will need citizens who understand science and can govern the way we use it.

Don't feel you have to know everything.

No one knows everything. It's important to understand the big ideas and principles of democracy, but if you don't remember all the details about which court does what, or how many people are on a city council, don't worry. You can re-learn those facts when you need them.

Get to know your neighbors.

Democracy depends on people having a sense of community. When neighbors know each other and help each other, they are more likely to participate in activities that make their neighborhoods safer, better places for kids to grow up to be good people.

Participate in the life of your community.

There are lots of activities that help democracy without really even involving politics or elections. Charities, religious groups, sports leagues, book clubs and arts organizations all contribute to making communities healthy places to live. This supports the work of government by helping us be a civilized society where people know how to get along with one another.

Think about the common good, and about individual liberty.

As human beings, we are all constantly trying to find the right balance between doing what we want to do, and doing what's best for the people around us. This is true in our family lives, in our schools, in our workplaces, and in our government. Being a good citizen requires thinking carefully about what's best for all of us, and what's best for each of us.

Lean towards optimism.

To make democracy succeed, we have to share the belief that human beings are capable of resolving differences peacefully, respecting each other, and putting aside selfish interests. But when people do things that are mean, corrupt, or hateful, it can make all of us wonder if democracy really works. When this happens, we have to remind ourselves of the progress our country has made. We have to stay focused on living up to the ideals in our constitution.

Think of yourself as a very powerful person.

You are. As a citizen of the world's only superpower, each American has more political power than a hundred citizens of a smaller, less prosperous democratic country – and thousands of times more powerful than citizens who live under corrupt or undemocratic governments. When we vote for President, we are voting for someone who will have an impact all over the world – not just on our fellow Americans. This is an enormous responsibility.

Question authority.

In fact, question everything. Democracy depends on people asking hard questions, and insisting on honest answers. If this country's founders hadn't questioned the authority of the British, we would still be curtsying to the Queen of England.

Don't waste time hating government.

Lots of people will tell you that government is no darn good, and that it wastes tax dollars and interferes with people's lives. Or they might say government is no darn good because it's all controlled by big-money interests and corporations. These statements may point out problems that need to be solved, but they sure don't help solve them. Complaining about something doesn't change it. And in a democracy, hating the government is a kind of self-hatred, because we're the ones who elect our government leaders.

Keep the faith.

What makes democracy work is that we all believe in it. If people stop believing in it, it will die. All the progress our country has made – from outlawing slavery to extending voting rights to everyone to making the 40-hour workweek a legal standard – happened because people believed that they could create change. They were right.

Appendix: A sampling of elected offcials, state agencies and departments

For a full listing see:
www.access.wa.gov
and click on "agencies"

Governor

PO Box 40002
Olympia, WA 98504-0002
360-902-4111
www.leg.wa.gov/governor

Lieutenant Governor

PO Box 40400
Olympia, WA 98504-0400
360-786-7700
www.ltgov.wa.gov

Secretary of State

PO Box 40220
Olympia, WA 98504-0220
360-902-4151
www.secstate.wa.gov

Attorney General

PO Box 40100
Olympia, WA 98504-0100
360-753-6200
www.wa.gov/ago

State Legislature

Representatives: PO Box 40600
Olympia WA, 98504-0600

Senators: PO Box 404,
Olympia WA, 98504
Hotline: 1-800-562-6000
www.access.wa.gov

Washington State Department of Agriculture

WSDA serves the people of Washington State by supporting the agricultural community and promoting consumer and environmental protection.
P.O. Box 42560
Olympia, WA 98504-2560
(360) 902-1800   TDD(360) 902-1996
www.agr.wa.gov/

Department of Corrections

As a partner with victims, communities and the criminal justice system, the Department enhances public safety, administers criminal sanctions of the courts and correctional programs, and provides leadership for the future of corrections in Washington state. The Department employs over 7,000 men and women to administer and

continued

supervise over 15,000 offenders housed in 13 institutions and 18 work training and pre-release facilities.

410 W 5th Ave
Olympia, WA 98504-1118
360-753-1573
www.doc.wa.gov

The Administrative Office of the Courts

This office provides educational resources including Judges in the Classroom, Informational Brochures, Judicial Education, Constitutional Information, Mock Trial Information and Washington State Court History.

P.O. Box 41170
Olympia, WA 98504-1170
Office (360) 753-3365
www.courts.wa.gov/

Department of Ecology

Ecology's mission is to protect, preserve and enhance Washington's environment, and promote the wise management of the state's air, land and water for the benefit of current and future generations. The goals are to prevent pollution, clean up pollution when it occurs, and support sustainable communities and natural resources.

P.O. Box 47600
Olympia, WA 98504-7600
www.ecy.wa.gov/

Washington State Employment Security Department

Employment Security helps people succeed throughout their working lives. The Department provides superior customer service to support workers during times of unemployment, connect job seekers with employers and provide business and individuals with the information and tools they need to adapt to a changing economy.

P.O. Box 9046
Olympia, WA 98507-9046
(360) 902-9301
www.fortress.wa.gov/esd/portal/

Office of Financial Management

Provides information, fiscal services and policy support that the Governor, Legislature and state agencies need to serve the people of Washington State, including development of capital and operating budget policy.

P.O. Box 43113
Olympia, WA 98504-3113
360-902-0555
TTY 360-902-0679
www.ofm.wa.gov

Northwest Indian Fisheries Commission

The tribes, who are working toward their own self-sufficiency, share the long-term goals of economic stability, renewable resources and regulatory certainty.

6730 Martin Way E.
Olympia, WA 98516
360 438-1180
www.nwifc.wa.gov

Washington Department of Fish and Wildlife

Fish and Wildlife has three major responsibilities: to develop and contribute to quality decision-making; to share responsibility for fish and wildlife through part-nerships with public and international entities, tribal leaders, public volunteers and service groups to share responsibility for fish and wildlife; to forge effective partnerships with landowners and land use decision makers in maintaining and enhancing habitat.

600 Capitol Way N.
Olympia, WA 98501-1091
Information: 360 902-2200
www.wdfw.wa.gov

Washington State Department of Health

Health services are population-based, focused on improving the health and status of the population, rather than simply treating individuals. This responsibility is shared by the Department of Health and 34 local health jurisdictions serving Washington's 39 counties.

P.O. Box 47890
Olympia, WA 98504-7890
http://www.doh.wa.gov/

Department of General Administration

General Administration contracts for food, equipment and services; delivers mail within state government; maintains state office buildings and grounds; manages public-works projects; helps food banks get meals to those in need; rents parking to agencies, employees and the public; rents GA-owned offices to state agencies; serves as the real estate agent for state government, and offers visitor services at the State Capitol.

Post Office Box 41000
Olympia, WA 98504-1000
(360) 902-7300
www.ga.wa.gov

Washington State Historical Society

The Society strives to make the study of history in Washington illuminating and inspiring by presenting diverse and compelling educational opportunities including exhibits, programs, and publications that make history relevant and alive; collects and preserves materials that form the fabric of Washington's history; and fosters a sense of identity and community by civic engagement and encourage the heritage activities of others.

1911 Pacific Avenue
Tacoma, WA 98402
1-888-238-4373
Information Line 253-272-9747
www.wshs.org

Commission on African American Affairs

The Commission encourages the development and implementation of policies, programs, and practices which are specifically intended to improve conditions affecting the cultural, social, economic, political, educational, health and general well-being of African American people at all levels throughout Washington State.

PO Box 40926
Olympia, WA 98504-0926
1-360-753-0127
www.caa.wa.gov

Commission on Asian Pacific American Affairs

The agency's mission is to improve the well-being of Asian Pacific Americans (APAs) by insuring their access to participation in the fields of government, business, education, and other areas.

1210 Eastside Street SE
Olympia, WA 98504-0925
1-360-586-9500
www.capaa.wa.gov

Commission on Hispanic Affairs

The Commission is charged with identifying and defining issues concerning the rights and needs of Washington State's Hispanic Community; advising the Governor and state agencies on the development of relevant policies, plans and programs that affect Hispanics; advising the legislature on issues of concern to the state's Hispanic community; and establishing relationships with state agencies, local governments, and members of the private sector.

P.O. Box 40924
Olympia, WA 98504-0924
Phone: (800) 443-0294
(360) 753-3159
www.cha.wa.gov

Governor's Office of Indian Affairs

Recognizing the importance of sovereignty, the Office affirms the government-to-government relationship and principles identified in the Centennial Accord to promote and enhance tribal self-sufficiency and serves to assist the state in developing policies consistent with those principles.

1210 Eastside St, 1st Floor
PO Box 40909
Olympia, WA 98504-0909
360 753-2411
www.goia.wa.gov

Office of the Insurance Commissioner

The Office assures that all authorized insurance companies meet and maintain rigid financial, legal, and other requirements for doing business in this state; licenses a number of insurance-related professionals, including agents, brokers and adjusters; protects the interest of consumers as its most important job through consumer guides and fact sheets to help Washington state residents be informed about their choices and rights when buying and using health coverage; offers the service of hundreds of trained volunteers statewide through the SHIBA Help Line for counseling, education and other assistance to consumers with health insurance and health care access issues and questions.

P.O. Box 40255
Olympia, WA 98504-0255
(360) 725-7080
or 1-800-562-6900 (in Washington only)
TDD (360) 586-0241
www.insurance.wa.gov

Washington State Department of Labor and Industries

L and I has programs to help employers meet safety and health standards and inspects workplaces when alerted to hazards; provides medical and limited wage-replacement coverage to workers who suffer job-related injuries and illness; helps ensure that workers are paid what they are owed, that children's and teens' work hours are limited, and that consumers are protected from unsound building practices.

PO Box 44000
Olympia, WA 98504-4000
Main Line: 1-800—547-8367
360-902-5800
TDD: 360-902-5797
http://www.lni.wa.gov/ English
http://www.lni.wa.gov/Spanish/ Spanish

Washington State Parks and Recreation Commission

The Washington State Parks and Recreation Commission acquires, operates, enhances and protects a diverse system of recreational, cultural, historical and natural sites. It fosters outdoor recreation and education statewide to provide enjoyment and enrichment for all, and a valued legacy to future generations.

P.O. Box 42650
7150 Cleanwater Lane
Olympia, WA 98504-2650
(360) 902-8844
www.parks.wa.gov

Public Disclosure Commission

PDC, originally created through initiative, provides timely and meaningful public access to information about the financing of political campaigns, lobbyist expenditures, and the financial affairs of public officials and candidates, and it ensures compliance with disclosure provisions, contribution limits, campaign practices and other campaign finance laws.

PO Box 40908
Olympia, WA 98504-0908
(360) 753-1111
Toll Free - 1-877-601-2828
www.pdc.wa.gov

Washington State Department of Natural Resources (Commissioner of Public Lands)

DNR is dedicated to providing professional, forward-looking stewardship of our state lands, natural resources, and environment; and providing leadership in creating a sustainable future for the trust lands and all citizens.

P.O. Box 47001
Olympia, WA 98504-7001
Phone: (360) 902-1004
FAX: (360) 902-1775
www.dnr.wa.gov

Governor's Office of the Family and Children's Ombudsman

The Office seeks to protect children and parents from harmful agency action or inaction, and to make agency officials and state policy makers aware of system-wide issues in the child protection and child welfare system so they can improve services.

6720 Fort Dent Way, Suite 240
Mail Stop TT-99
Tukwila, WA 98188
(206) 439-3870 • 1-800-571-7321
(206) 439-3789/TTY
www.governor.wa.gov/ofco

Office of the Superintendent of Public Instruction

IThe Office of Superintendent of Public Instruction, in collaboration with educators, students, families, local communities, business, labor, and government, leads, supports, and oversees K-12 education, ensuring the success of all learners.

PO Box 47200
Olympia, WA 98504-7200
(360) 725-6000
TTY (360) 664-3631
www.k12.wa.us

Washington State Department of Social and Health Services

DSHS provides programs for children, families and people with special needs and those needing long-term care, in partnerships with families, community groups, private providers, other government agencies, and through foster parents, neighbors, and citizens.

Constituent Services 1-800-737-0617
www1.dshs.wa.gov

Washington State Department of Transportation

The Washington State Department of Transportation keeps people and business moving by operating and improving the state transportation systems vital to our taxpayers and communities.

310 Maple Park Avenue SE
PO Box 47300
Olympia WA 98504-7300
Information 360-705-7000
www.wsdot.wa.gov

Washington State Patrol

The Washington State Patrol provides public safety services to everyone where they live, work, travel, and play, making a difference every day.

PO Box 42600
Olympia WA 98504-2600
(360) 753-6540
www.wsp.wa.gov

Resource book on the Washington State constitution:

The Washington State Constitution: A Reference Guide by Robert F. Utter and Hugh Spitzer, Greenwood Publishing Group/Pacific Northwest.

This is an easy to read, easy to use reference guide, available at most libraries and from online booksellers.

For further information and supplementary material visit:

www.washingtonvoter.org

(the League of Women Voters of Washington non-partison voter service web site)